THE "CUTTY

THE LAST OF THE FAMOUS

Being a description of the Hull, Deck Fittings,
and Rigging of this famous ship, together with
a detailed account of the building of a scale
model, which will shortly be added to the collection at the Science Museum, South Kensington

BY

C. NEPEAN LONGRIDGE

Author of "Anatomy of Nelson's Ships."

TWO VOLUMES IN ONE

VoL. I.—An account of the ship itself, with
plans and full instructions for building the hull,
bulwarks, and deck fittings of a scale model

FULLY ILLUSTRATED

EDWARD W. SWEETMAN COMPANY

NEW YORK

1959

THE "CUTTY SARK"

"CUTTY SARK"

"CUTTY SARK"

"CUTTY SARK"

"CUTTY SARK"

"CUTTY SARK"

"CUTTY SARK"

"CUTTY SARK"

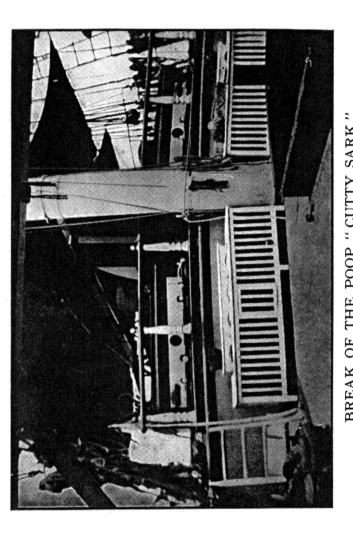

BREAK OF THE POOP "CUTTY SARK."

DECK OF " CUTTY SARK," 1922.

"CUTTY SARK"

PREFACE

I HAVE written this book in the hope that it may help other amateurs who are interested in the fascinating hobby of modelling ships, and also be of use to those who want to know something about the details of a sailing ship's arrangements.

Three years ago, when the desire to build a model of a sailing ship took possession of me, I tried to find a book which described one, from what I may call the anatomical point of view. I was soon informed, on very good authority, that no such book existed in the English language. The knowledge, of course, is still to be found. I have gleaned from books and pictures, from talks, ashore and afloat, with men who have served their time in sail, from museum models, and from visits to several of the ships which still sail the seas.

The main source of my information, however, has been the *Cutty Sark*, and owing to the courtesy of her owners I have been able to spend several days on board of her in Falmouth Harbour, with a camera, a foot rule, and a notebook.

This book is founded on the facts so collected. I have no doubt that the book would have been written better by a seaman than by one who has not been trained to the sea. The fear of making stupid mistakes has deterred me from venturing to write anything about the working of a ship, except where it became necessary to explain some of her gear. More than one seafaring friend has, however, passed these parts of my manuscript without criticism.

Although models of the *Cutty Sark* are so many and

varied that, as a prototype, she is a somewhat hackneyed subject, I decided to build a model of her because authentic material for a scale model is available from photographs, measurements, and inspection of the ship, which make it possible to build a more accurate model of her than of any other ship of her time.

From the æsthetic point of view a scale model of the ship cannot fail to be a beautiful thing. Many lovers of ships agree that the tea clippers built between 1860 and 1870 were the loveliest ships that ever sailed. Of that swift and graceful sisterhood the *Cutty Sark* alone survives; she is as beautiful as any of them, and though years and the sea have somewhat battered her beauty, it is of that imperishable type which will always rise triumphant; and it inspires one to good work.

The book contains a description of her hull, deck work, and rigging, sufficiently detailed, documented, and complete to enable anyone to produce a scale model. Incidentally, as most of the clipper ships had a strong family likeness, the information given will be found to be useful in building models of other ships.

I am painfully aware that the best amateur cannot approach professional work in point of merit, but I do think that amateur work can always show the very great virtue of sincerity, which will lift a ship model to the level of a work of art. Anyone can build the model described in these pages if he really wants to do so; patience and a determination to achieve are far more important than skill—that will inevitably follow.

In doing the work, if one takes it seriously, difficulties will doubtless occur. These difficulties are one of the most fascinating things about it for the amateur. Quite certainly, there is always a way to overcome them, and in the exercise of one's intelligence to find that way will be found one of the great satisfactions and pleasures of the work. But many people nowadays are in a hurry.

Together, therefore, with the description of the ship I have given details of the methods used in building the model. The difficulties have not been glossed over; the dodges used to circumvent them may make the professional worker smile, should he happen to read this book, but I can definitely state that these dodges work. Here, again, the methods of construction of the hull and details of the deck work and rigging are applicable to models of other ships, so that I have every hope that these volumes will be of real use to the ship modeller in general.

The second volume will contain the complete, original specification of the ship. This valuable and historic document is treasured by the owners of the ship, who, realising the very great interest it has for all students of our maritime history, have very kindly allowed it to be published,

Mr J. GILBERT, Naval Instructor on the *Cutty Sark*.

and so have added to the great debt we already owe them.

It is a great pleasure to acknowledge my indebtedness to many people who have helped me in the production of this book. Space will not allow me to mention them all by name. Foremost among them I place Mr J. Gilbert—whom you see here, as the papers say—the naval instructor and general father and mother of the *Cutty Sark*. I am sure my long postal bombardment of questions would have annoyed anyone less genial than Mr Gilbert, but he has never failed to send me any information or measurement that I wanted. More than my thanks are due to Mr Maurice Denny, of Dumbarton, who has taken a kindly interest in the book, and has provided many of the photographs and drawings, and to Mr G. S. Laird Clowes, of the Science Museum, whose foreword precedes this preface, and who is, I may truthfully say, really responsible for the model in virtue of the encouragement he has given me from its earliest inception. I wish also to express my gratitude to Mr Roy Hands, whose semi-diagrammatic line drawings will, I am sure, be appreciated by all my readers ; to Mr Opie, of Falmouth, whose beautiful photograph of the ship adorns the first page of this volume, and to the *Daily Mirror*, by whose courtesy I am enabled to print others of the photographs.

Lastly, I am under a great obligation to Mr Harold Underhill, whose drawings are so well known. He has not only very kindly permitted me to include a set of these drawings in the book, but has gone so far as to alter his original drawings in order to modify certain details which were not in agreement with my text.

C. NEPEAN LONGRIDGE.

January 1933.

NOTE.—All being well, the model of the *Cutty Sark* described in this book will be on exhibition in the Science Museum at South Kensington in October 1933.

CONTENTS

LIST OF ILLUSTRATIONS

FOLDING PLATES.

The *Cutty Sark*

INTRODUCTION

THE LAST OF THE FAMOUS TEA CLIPPER SHIPS.

In the year 1869 two events occurred which are of interest to the reader of this book. The Empress Eugénie, with the strains of Verdi's new opera, " Aïda," titivating her delicate ears, opened the Suez Canal, and a small firm, Scott & Linton, started to build at Dumbarton a ship to the order of Captain John Willis. Shipowning in those days was not an affair of large public companies. There were many individuals who owned and managed their ships, and took the greatest pride and personal interest in them. John Willis was one such ; he was brought up to the sea, and had sailed in, and commanded, some of his father's ships before he launched out as an owner on his own account. He was a bachelor, a rich man, and very good-looking, if one may judge from the photograph of him in Lubbock's book. One can imagine that he and old Mr Jolyon Forsyte, who must have taken an acute interest in the doings of the tea clippers, made a convivial pair of cronies.

It has been the life ambition of many men to win the Derby. John Willis, like all his other shipowning friends and rivals, hoped and schemed to win another blue ribbon, the annual tea race home from China. They spent their money and built their lovely ships with that sporting end in view ; incidentally, they were close-fisted business men. Few of them, however, were far-seeing enough to under-stand the significance of the " ditch in the sand," and of

the "steam kettles" that soon began to frequent it.
Willis got hold of a young designer called Hercules Linton,
who had been trained under Hall, of Aberdeen; they put
their heads together and evolved the lines of a new ship,
designed with a view to out-sailing any contemporary
ship. Willis had a favourite ship called the *Tweed*,
magnificently built of teak. She was built in India, and
started life as a paddle steamer; her lines, it is said, were
taken off an old French frigate.

It is generally stated that Hercules Linton took off
the lines of the *Tweed* and used them as the foundation
of his design for the new ship. Captain Millett, who
served his time on both the *Tweed* and the *Cutty Sark*,
assures me that this is not the case. The lines of the
Tweed were taken off, but not by Linton or for the *Cutty
Sark*. It was Maudsley, Son, & Field who took off her
lines, and used them for the construction of the *Blackadder*
and the *Hallowe'en*, two iron sister ships which Willis
ordered about the same time that the *Cutty Sark* was on
the stocks.

The entire credit for the design of the *Cutty Sark*
belongs to Linton alone. He embodied in it the cream of
all clipper-ship experience; and the ship was the sublim-
ated essence of the best features of all the clipper ships
which had preceded her. To this he added a feature which
every inquiry I have hitherto made proves to be unique,
and that is the angular fore foot. The deadwood was
not cut away in the usual graceful curve. I may be making
a mistake in saying that this fore foot was unique, but no
drawing I have seen of her contemporaries shows this
feature. There is no doubt that this mordant fore foot
accounted for the extraordinary capacity of the ship to
eat her way to windward. There were not wanting wise-
acres who shook their heads and prophesied that this
unusual accentuation of the forward deadwood would
cause the ship to be constantly missing stays; they were

wrong, however, for experience proved that she was extremely handy in going about.

The entrance was extremely sharp, but the midship section with its squarish bilges and comparative fullness compensated the lack of bearing forward. The underwater portion of the after-body was fairly fine, but Linton insisted on imposing upon it a more powerful counter

THE " CUTTY SARK " UNDER SAIL.
From a photograph taken by Captain Woodget in 1886.
(Nautical Photo Agency.)

than was usual at the time. His skilled draughtsmanship succeeded in blending these three factors into a very sweet-lined whole. I have no doubt that in later years Captain Woodget, in running down his easting, often had occasion to bless Linton for this buoyant counter, which lifted the ship clear of many a sea which might otherwise have pooped her. The extremely sharp entrance made her, like all her sisters, an uncomfortably wet ship ;

indeed, it used to be said of these clippers, that when outward bound to Australia they took a dive off the Cape and came up to breathe at Cape Leeuwin. In this connection it is interesting to look at the model, in the Science Museum, of the *Torrens*, a later ship (1875) but still of the clipper type. She had the reputation of being one of the driest ships ever built. Comparing her entrance with that of the *Cutty Sark*, it is at once obvious how much more bearing she has forward, to keep her from diving. This tendency to increase the forward lifting power is being carried to great lengths in modern design. Quite recently I saw two ships in Rotterdam which had no bows at all in the ordinary sense of the word. The forward end was cut right away in a rounded inclined plane, somewhat like the end of a Thames lighter; the idea, I suppose, being to reduce resistance by allowing the entrance almost to skim over the water like a hydroplane. I should imagine, however, that in a head sea the hammering must be terrific.

In 1869 the most popular form of shipbuilding was the composite hull. Shipowners were on the whole a conservative body, and they could not quite suddenly desert wood for iron. The composite ship was the transitional compromise between the two. The hull was built of iron frames, deck beams, and stringers, with a timber keel and a skin of teak. This form of construction was more or less forced on builders for two reasons; firstly, the supply of suitable timber was getting very short, and secondly, the necessary size of the timber framing reduced very considerably the carrying capacity of a ship. Iron framing of commensurate strength was in illimitable supply, and occupied but a fraction of the space taken up by timber framing.

Scott & Linton accepted the contract to build her at £17 a ton,* a low price even in those days. Moreover, Willis apparently had the right to send one of his own

* The original contract is in the Dumbarton Free Library.

men to supervise the construction, and to reject any material which he considered unsuitable. Captain Moodie, one of Willis' most trusted commanders, was selected for this duty. His unimpeachable loyalty to his owner's interests may, or may not, have been the cause of the builders' bankruptcy before the ship was completed, but it was certainly due to his tireless vigilance that the *Cutty Sark* left the stocks with one of the most perfectly built hulls, in regard to both material and workmanship, that ever took the water.

On the failure of Scott & Linton, the firm of Denny Brothers, of Dumbarton, finished the ship, and she was launched on 23rd November 1869. Lubbock states that on 21st December she was towed to Greenock to be masted and rigged, and left Greenock on 13th January 1870. It is surprising to learn from these dates how quickly a ship was rigged in those days. She left London on her maiden voyage to China on 15th February 1870.

The origin of the ship's peculiar name has been somewhat of a puzzle to many. " Cutty sark " is Scotch for " short shirt." Captain Willis was a North Country man, and gave many of his ships names which recalled his youth, such as *Tweed*, *Blackadder*, *Hallowe'en*, etc. Apparently he admired Burns' works, and in particular the poem, " Tam o' Shanter," which relates how Farmer Tam was coming home one stormy night from market on his old grey mare Maggie. Tam had had a skinful, and was in a ripe condition to see things. He stumbled upon a witches' revel ; one of the witches was young, but let Burns continue :—

> " But here my muse her wing maun cour ;
> Sic flights are far beyond her pow'r ;
> To sing how Nannie lap and flang
> (A souple jade she was, an' strang),
> An' how Tam stood, like ane bewitch'd
> An' thought his very een enriched ;

Ev'n Satan glower'd, and fidg'd fu' fain
An' hotched an' blew wi' might an' main :
Till first ae caper, syne anither,
Tam tint his reason a' thegither
An' roars out. ' Weel done, Cutty sark.'
An' in an instant a' was dark."

It is not my purpose here to go into any history of the ship's voyages. The ground has been very amply and ably covered by Lubbock in his " Log of the *Cutty Sark*," and I have no doubt that most of my readers are well acquainted with the book. She was unlucky in her China voyages, and did not succeed in winning the coveted blue ribbon of the seas. The Suez Canal and the steamers between them very soon wrested the cream of the China trade from the clippers. The foundations of the great Blue Funnel Line were laid on their ashes. Alfred Holt's early steamers were provided with a compound engine, the high pressure being on the top of the low-pressure cylinder, thus saving considerable space for cargo and earning princely freights. Thirty years ago I saw one of these old steamers in Eastern waters, still earning money under Chinese ownership.

It was in the Australian wool trade, under Captain Woodget, that the *Cutty Sark* won her real fame and made her greatest runs, although her sail plan had been severely cut down. The records of all these runs are given by Lubbock. She was by no means the fastest ship that ever sailed, but it can, I think, be claimed for her that she was the fastest ship *of her size* ever built. In 1855 the great Black-baller, *Lightning*, is said to have run a distance of 436 nautical miles in twenty-four hours as against the *Cutty Sark's* best run of 360, and the *James Baines* is reputed to have logged 21 knots. But these were bigger and more powerful ships, and it is only fair to state that the authenticity of all these phenomenal runs is gravely doubted by competent observers.

Mr Denny has recently made some interesting trials

in his experimental tank at Dumbarton. He found that it would require approximately 3000 h.p. to drive the *Cutty Sark* at load draught at a speed of 16 knots, a speed which she is said to have attained ; in other words, her sails developed no less than 3000 h.p.

In 1895 Willis sold the *Cutty Sark* to the Portuguese firm of Ferreira. She was renamed after the firm and sailed away into oblivion for many years. Occasionally she turned up in an English port, and an enterprising reporter might remember her fame and send his paper a few paragraphs about her. During the war she was dismasted off the Cape, and was re-rigged as a barquentine in Cape Town ; and then, in 1922, Captain and Mrs Dowman bought her back at a fancy price, and so restored her to British ownership, and earned the undying gratitude of all ship-lovers in these islands. Entirely at their own—and, I can imagine, very great—expense they have masted and rigged her as she was at the time of her maiden voyage, and have for some years trained on board of her scores of boys for both the Royal Navy and the Merchant Service. A suit of sails has been made for her, and the day may yet come when once more she will spread her wings and sail away into the sunrise.

THE "CUTTY SARK."

CHAPTER I.

THE HULL.

The Drawings.—Before beginning the actual work it is necessary to study carefully the drawing. The plans of a ship's hull are contained in three separate drawings, and each of these drawings is complementary to the others. These drawings will be found in a folder at the end of this volume. An expert is able to visualise the lines of a hull from the drawings, but we novices and amateurs seldom attain such proficiency, nor indeed is it necessary that we should do so. We can, however, by understanding what the drawings mean, and by working to them, reproduce the lines of the ship absolutely accurately.

The drawings have this in common : they are divided up by a series of vertical and horizontal lines, and the actual lines of the ship are drawn within this system of ordinates.

The Sheer Plan.—The first drawing to study is the sheer plan, which shows the profile of the hull looked at from the side. This is divided first by a series of horizontal lines parallel with the water-line. Drawings made for model work generally have these horizontal lines spaced an inch, or half an inch, apart, because so much model shipbuilding is done on what is called the " Bread and Butter System," and it is a convenience to have the horizontal lines thus equally spaced so that the planks out of which the hull is to be constructed may all be planed down to the same thickness. The sheer plan is also divided up by a series of vertical lines spaced at some arbitrary interval apart, such as 3 in. These lines are called the station lines, and are always numbered. The outline of the hull is contained within these lines. If the hull, being correctly constructed, were to be sawn into two equal halves by a cut running fore and aft, the outline of the cut surface ought to correspond with the outline as shown by the sheer plan.

The Buttock Lines.—The sheer plan also shows, inside the outline of the hull, three other curved lines running in the same general direction as the curved outline of the hull. These lines are the buttock lines. Imagine you had a ship's hull carved out of a solid block of wood with the fore and aft middle line marked on its deck surface. Draw lines parallel with the middle line, 1, 2, and 3 in. outside the middle line. Now, in imagination of course, saw through the length of the hull vertically, along these lines. You would get a series of slices of hull of varying shapes. The buttock lines in the drawing show the shape of these imaginary slices.

The Half-breadth Plan.—The second drawing is the half-breadth plan. It shows the outline of the hull at each horizontal plane as divided by the horizontal lines in the sheer drawing. These outlines are all curved lines : they are separate and distinct at the fore and after ends, but amidships they tend to run into one another and become somewhat confusing. When, however, the lines are read in connection with the two other drawings their significance is plain. The half-breadth plan also shows the station lines, and from these station lines the breadth of the hull at any point on any of the horizontal planes can be ascertained—at any point, that is, on a station line. At any other point the breadth can also be taken, by measuring with a pair of dividers the distance from the middle line to the desired point.

The Body Plan.—The third drawing is called the body plan. It is divided again by the horizontal lines and also by a series of vertical lines. The central vertical line is the middle line of the ship. The other vertical lines are the buttock lines seen end on. The curved lines are the station lines. If the solid block hull referred to above were sawn into a series of slices transversely at the station lines, their outlines would be as represented in the body plan. The lines in the right-hand side of the drawing show the lines of the forward half and those on the left-hand side show the after half of the hull. The curved line along the top of this drawing indicates the sheer, which is the long, flowing, fore and aft curved line along the upper margin of the hull : the sheer is also shown in the sheer plan. The sheer line is one of the most beautiful of all the lines of a ship : well designed, the sheer line can impart grace and nobility to a ship ; on the other hand, a badly drawn sheer can make a ship positively ugly. Read what Masefield, a man who knows both ships and beauty, has to say about the lovely sheer line of the *Wanderer*.

With these three drawings you have every dimension necessary to construct the hull. The scale of the drawing has to be taken into consideration. If the drawing is to $\frac{1}{4}$-in. scale, that means that $\frac{1}{4}$ in. of the drawing represents 1 ft. of the real ship. Most working drawings for ships are, I believe, drawn on this scale. If your model is going to be on the same scale, you can work directly from the plans, but if your drawing is $\frac{1}{4}$ in. and your model $\frac{1}{8}$ in., or vice versa, the drawing has to be reproduced to correspond. I believe there are various ways of doing this. I must confess that hitherto I have taken the shortest and, I think, the best way for an amateur to tackle this difficulty, and that is to find a professional draughtsman and get him to do the job.

The Scale of the Model.—Here I might say a word or two with regard to the scale of the model. It all depends on what you are aiming at. If you want an ornament for your home, and something which is a bit more than the ordinary ornament, space must be considered. Few of us live in houses which can comfortably accommodate a large glass case. From the ornamental point of view, a model of a 200-ft. ship on $\frac{1}{8}$-in. scale would be 25 in. long ; most of our houses can manage that. The overall length of the *Cutty Sark* when rigged is 280 ft., that is 35 in. on $\frac{1}{8}$-in. scale, and 70 in. or just on 6 ft. long, on $\frac{1}{4}$-in. scale. With the glass case, even the $\frac{1}{8}$-in. scale model is a fairly bulky object, and not one that should be often moved about. For the home the $\frac{1}{8}$-in. scale is undoubtedly the better, but it is only on the $\frac{1}{4}$-in. that the detail can be reproduced faithfully by the average amateur. There are very few details, indeed, which do not lend themselves to reproduction on this scale, and it gives one an opportunity for the exercise of whatever talent and sincerity one possesses, and if one only sticks consistently to the scale sizes, the fittings and so on do seem to belong to the ship. It is better to leave out a fitting altogether rather than stick on pieces which are hopelessly over scale. Therefore, for a show or exhibition model the $\frac{1}{4}$-in. scale has come to be recognised as the best.

Any of my readers who are acquainted with the work of Mr Norman Ough may be inclined to disagree with these remarks. Mr Ough works to $\frac{1}{16}$-in. scale. For meticulous and complete accuracy of detail his work stands in a class by itself alone, but then Mr Ough is a genius, and he has shown us that even on $\frac{1}{16}$-in. scale the minutest detail of a complicated warship can be represented faithfully. Anyone who is curious to see to what heights ship modelling can rise should make a point of visiting the United Service Institution Museum in Whitehall to look at his latest model, that of the aircraft carrier *Glorious*. It is simply marvellous.

Material for the Hull.—The question of the scale having been decided, the wood out of which the hull is to be constructed must now be procured. It must be dry and well seasoned, it should be as free from knots as possible, straight-grained, and kindly in working. Yellow pine is the best wood to use, but it is scarce, difficult to come by, and expensive. Oregon pine is a good wood to use. A cabinetmaker provided me with the wood for my model; it was very well seasoned and easy to work. He simply called it "pine." I do not know what, if any, particular brand of pine it was, nor did he.

The Bread and Butter System.—The bread and butter system of building was mentioned above. Before proceeding further, an explanation of what is meant by this system may be given. The hull is constructed of planks about an inch thick laid upon the top of each other and glued together; the advantages of building the hull in this way are great. In the first place, it is easier to obtain timber of suitable size and quality; and secondly, by marking out each plank separately and working to the lines marked out, it is almost impossible to produce an asymmetrical hull. For the amateur, therefore, I should advise the bread and butter method of building every time.

Having decided upon and obtained the wood, it must be sawn into the requisite number of planks. Each plank must be rather more than the full length and width of the corresponding horizontal plane in the drawing, and must be planed down exactly to the necessary thickness. Unless the builder is a skilful carpenter, I think it pays to have this preliminary work done in a competent woodworking shop. Then you will get all the planks absolutely squared and surfaced to the exact dimensions all over. The planks should be $9\frac{1}{2}$ in. wide and 1 in. thick finished. The bottom plank need not be more than 7 in. wide. Have a groove

$\frac{5}{16}$ in. wide and $\frac{3}{8}$ in. deep ploughed along the' centre of the bottom plank to take the keel, which should be a strip of oak or pine $\frac{5}{16}$ in. wide and $\frac{3}{4}$ in. deep and about 4 ft. long.

Marking Out.—Now comes the important process of marking out. Time spent over this is not wasted, as it is the foundation of the whole symmetry of the ship, and if you can be quite certain that your marks are correct it saves you a lot of trouble later on. The lines should be marked with a sharp scriber and afterwards lightly pencilled with a hard, sharp pencil. A tested square, a reliable straight-edge, a pair of dividers, and a parallel ruler are required.

To test a square, lay it up against a bit of paper and draw a pencil line along the blade, then turn it over and draw a second line. If these lines diverge the square is not true.

The Centre Line.—Begin by marking out the centre line of each plank. Mark the centre line, not only on the top and bottom surface of the plank, but over the ends of them as well. When you have marked all the planks, stack them on top of each other with their sides flush, and see if the centre lines down the ends of the planks are dead in line and vertical. If the planks pass this test you can be satisfied that the centre lines are correct, if not, mistakes must be rectified before proceeding further.

The Station Lines.—The station lines at right angles to the centre line must be marked in 3 in. apart. With the planks squarely stacked up and all flush, select a point about the middle of the centre line of the top plank. With the square scribe a line accurately round the top and sides of the stack of planks. This line will, of course, be at right angles to the centre line, and will be the middle station line. Now take your top plank, and from the point where the middle station line crosses the centre line mark off the necessary number of station points 3 in. apart along the centre line fore and aft. This must be done accurately. The dividers will not do it, as the points tend to sink into the wood. If you have not got a long metal ruler, prepare a batten of $\frac{1}{32}$-in. three-ply wood, mark it off in 3 in., and use it for marking off the station points on all the planks. Check the points after marking them, turn the plank over, and from the scribed line on its side, which represents the middle station line, find with the help of the square the corresponding point on the centre line of the under side of the plank. Fom this point again mark out the station points fore and aft, and with the square scribe the station lines round the whole of the plank. If the woodworking shop has planed up the planks true, and your measurements are accurate, the square station lines round the plank will come true. Do the same thing with all the planks, and number each station line top and bottom. The square line originally scribed down the sides of the planks will give you the guide for the middle station in each case, so that when all the planks have been scribed and stacked up again there should be a series of vertical lines 3 in. apart along the sides of the stack.

Dowelling the Planks.—From now on it is essential that the planks should retain their relative positions, and therefore it is a good thing to dowel them temporarily together. After consulting the drawing, choose a spot at the end of each plank where the dowels will not inter-fere with anything, drill a $\frac{1}{8}$-in. hole $\frac{1}{2}$ in. deep at each spot and insert the dowels. They will be, of course, in the middle line and just under an inch long. Stack up the planks again with the dowels in position in order to test the accuracy of the dowelling, and if you find that all the sides are square and flush you can go on to the next proceeding.

Marking Out the Half-breadth Lines.—This consists in marking out on each station line the distance between the centre line and the outside of the ship at each particular point. These distances can be obtained from either the body plan or the half-breadth plan. It is easier to use the body plan, because one is apt to make mistakes with the confusing lines of the half-breadth plan. Using dividers with screw adjustment, take off from the plan the half-breadth at any station you like. Put one point of the dividers lightly in the dot in the centre line at that station, and with the other point mark the half-breadth at the outer end of the station line. Lift the dividers and make a similar mark at the opposite end of the line. The two marks should then be equidistant from the centre line. Draw a circle in red ink round each mark so that they are not lost. Every station line on the top and bottom of each plank must be marked off in this way. The half-breadths on the station lines will not be the same on the top and bottom aspects of the planks owing to the curvature of the hull. Do not rush this job ; unless you are concentrating your mind upon it you can very easily make mistakes. When all the stations are marked, take a ruler and draw straight lines between adjacent red-inked dots. You will then have the outline of the hull on each plank— not the exact outline, because the station lines have been joined by straight lines. Properly speaking, the half-breadth points on the station lines should be joined by curved lines. This is done by a thin, springy batten called a " spline," but it requires a good deal of skill, and is really not worth the time, provided you remember that these lines do not represent the real outlines of the ship. The outline, however, must pass through the red-inked half-breadth points on the station lines. You will notice, of course, that the lines on the bottom aspect of one plank correspond exactly with the lines on the top aspect of the plank immediately below it. All the wood outside of these lines will be cut away.

Cutting Out the Inside of the Planks.—Now turn the stack of planks upside down and remove the slotted bottom plank. Draw in red ink another line about half an inch inside the lines on the bottom aspect of each plank. This line is the guide for cutting out the inside of the planks. Where the surface of the hull is very much curved, as at the stern, allow more than half an inch. The dowels must lie outside the red line. Then take your planks to the woodworking shop and have the inside sawn out by a jig-saw along the red-ink lines. When you get them back, draw in with the square the station lines on the inside sawn edge, so that when the dowels are replaced and the planks stacked up again you will have the station lines visible on the inside of your model. The inside will be in steps. Do not pare down these steps with a chisel but leave them as they are.

Roughing Out the Hull.—Now saw away the superfluous wood from the outside of each plank, using the lines on the upper surface of the planks as a guide. Some faint resemblance to the shape of a ship will begin to emerge when the planks are once more joined together.

The lower edges of the planks project and have to be cut away to fit the upper edges of planks beneath. These edges cannot be planed straight off, otherwise the surface of the hull would be a collection of flats. Gouges, chisels, and a spokeshave must be used for the work of shaping the hull, and it is essential to make a set of templates.

The Templates.—To make these templates, make a tracing of a station line from the body plan, and include in the tracing, first the horizontal base line, and secondly the vertical line on the outside of the body plan. These two lines are, of course, at right angles. The tracing is transferred by means of a piece of carbon paper to whatever material is being used for the template, which is then cut out to the line. It is obviously of the first importance that the curved line of the template should retain its proper position relatively to the horizontal and vertical

lines of the body plan. It is not necessary to make
a template for every section, especially towards the
middle of the ship, but every section at the bow and
the stern—say the end five—should have a template
made.

Shaping the Hull.—Holding the job while working on
it is a difficulty. I sat astride of my planks and worked on
them in that way. I can only give general instructions
about shaping the hull. You must have a good idea of
the shape you are aiming at in your mind's eye. Rough
it out with a large gouge ; do not attempt any sort of
finishing touches until you have the whole roughed out.
You will find the stern the most difficult part. You must
rely on you own skill and determination to get the thing
right. The templates must be used at their proper stations
as guides, and for comparing the two sides. Have the
keel, with the station lines marked off, in its groove when
trying on a template, and see that it touches the keel at
its correct station as well as the station line on the top
plank. As the work progresses, and the lovely shape of
the ship grows under your hands, you will begin to love
it for its grace and beauty, and your determination will
grow to give it the best that is in you : it is the pride
of the artist. While being reasonably careful, do not
be too afraid of making mistakes ; cut at it, do not
scratch at it here and there. Mistakes can be rectified.
I made one quite bad flat on my model and built it
up again.

When you have got the shape roughed out and the
templates really fit, have a good look at it from various
angles in a good light. The eye is a marvellous judge of
symmetry.

The Stem.—At this stage it is well to make the stem
piece. From the profile plan of the ship make a tracing of the
stem ; include the upper edge where it touches and supports
the bowsprit. On this tracing draw a line parallel with and

$\frac{3}{8}$ in. behind its after edge. Transfer this tracing to a piece of 3-ply wood $\frac{1}{8}$ in. thick, and cut out the stem piece to this pattern. On this stem piece draw lines parallel with and $\frac{3}{8}$ in. in front of its after edge. With a sharp knife cut down to, but not through, the centre layer of the 3-ply on these lines, and remove the outer layers. The centre layer dovetails into the stem of the ship (*v.* Fig. 1).

Raking the Stem and Stern. — Now cut down the stem ends of your planks to the rake of the stem shown in the drawing. Doing this removes the vertical centre lines. Here you have to be very careful. You have to make a saw cut down the centre line to receive the centre layer of the

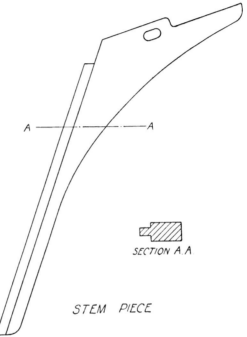

SECTION A.A

STEM PIECE

FIG. 1.—The Stem Piece cut from 3-ply wood and dovetailing into the planks of the hull.

3-ply stem piece. Take the planks apart and mark out the centre line again from the centre lines which are intact on the upper and lower surfaces of the planks. Start the saw cut on each with a tenon saw. Put the two bottom planks together and deepen the cut a little; then the third, and so on, till your saw is running true through the whole length of the cut. This accomplished, let the fore end of the keel piece project a little, and with the saw running in the groove extend the cut into the keel piece. The hull, the stem, and the keel will now all hold together. The stem piece will project upwards a good deal, because the sheer pieces have not been put on as yet.

The stern has a very slight rake, and this should be cut. The end of the keel projects a little beyond the stern post, and is bevelled.

Smoothing the Hull.—The hull is now ready for smoothing. A plane, judiciously used, will do a good deal of the work amidships. Notice that the greatest beam of the ship is below the water-line; above the water-line the sides of the hull fall inwards slightly. This falling inwards is called the tumble-home; it amounts to $\frac{1}{4}$ in. at the rail, and is one of the things which make a model look like a real ship.

The more curly parts at the bow and stern can be smoothed with a wood rasp, a sharp scraper, and sandpaper. Be careful now not to make any flats, and frequently inspect the work to ensure its symmetry. As the surface of the hull is not going to show, it is waste of time to work for a paintable surface.

On looking at the model from the side it is obvious that there is something wrong with it. It has as yet no sheer. The sheer is the long, flowing curved line that runs along the rail from the bow of a ship to her stern when looked at sideways. So far, the upper surface of the model is parallel with the keel, and it is better to fix the planks permanently together before the sheer pieces are put on.

Glueing the Planks Together.—Take the two uppermost pieces, hold them up to the light, and see if any daylight shows along the line where they touch each other. If they are not in perfect apposition rub down the high spots with sand-paper. Prepare a flat surface on which to lay the pieces when glued, and have handy some heavy weights and three pieces of board about 12 in. by 6 in. There are various brands of glue powder on the market which, when mixed with cold water, make a very strong joint. Glue up the two pieces, including the dowels, lay them on the flat surface, put the three pieces of board across, and on these lay the weights. If some adequate clamps are available use them instead of weights, but use them in conjunction with boards to spread the pressure and avoid crushing the hull. The pieces should be left undisturbed for twenty-four hours; then glue together two more pieces, and when set hard glue the four in the same way. The dowels act as a register for the right position and also strengthen the joints. Leave the bottom plank to the last. Owing to the curvature of its under surface it is not so easy to squeeze it down with weights, but the difficulty can be got over by laying a couple of round rods, about the size of broomsticks, on either side of the keel and tying them loosely together so that they do not roll off. The weights can be adjusted on these rods so that they exert an even pressure over the joint between the bottom plank and the next one. Do not glue in the stem piece at present.

The Sheer Pieces.—It is now necessary to make the sheer pieces fore and aft. Before doing so read the section on housing the masts. The topmost horizontal line in the drawing is the base of the sheer pieces, and this line is at the level of the main deck somewhere about the middle or waist of the ship. The deck itself sweeps upwards to the bow and slightly less towards the stern, corresponding roughly with the sheer line. Measure the height of the sheer from the drawing at the various stations and cut the pieces out of a plank. Plane them down to the approximate thickness and fit them to the ship with dowels; do not attempt at present to get the correct concave curvatures on their upper surfaces. When firmly, though temporarily, dowelled in position, work the outer

surface to correspond with the rest of the surfaces of the
ship. At the bows there is a considerable amount of flare
or overhang, and the templates will guide you here. When
you have shaped the pieces satisfactorily, take them off,
mark a line $\frac{5}{8}$ in. from the edge, and saw out the redundant
wood, leaving the pieces horseshoe-shaped. The dowels
must be in the part left. Fit them to the ship again and
glue them down, and then make a template of the sheer
from the drawing. This template is better made in two
pieces, one for the fore end and one for the after end of
the ship, and it should be made of thin wood, such as
veneer or ply wood. It is not at all easy to work the
slight concave curve of the sheer equally on both sides,
so take time about it, and test the work frequently with
the template. A spokeshave set fine is the best tool to
use. To finish off, roll a piece of sand-paper on a stick
long enough to touch both sides. Holding this in both
hands, stand in front of your ship and rub it up and down
with steady long strokes. The sand-paper will fine off
the ends of the sheer pieces where they tail away to nothing
amidships.

The saw cut made to take the stem must now be
extended to the sheer piece, and the centre line marked
clearly fore and aft.

The Stem Rabbet.—If you intend to plank the top
sides of your hull, it is necessary now to form the rabbet
at the stem. Take a scrap bit of 3-ply and cut away the
two outer layers as you did when making the stem piece.
Fit this into the saw cut temporarily. With a fine chisel
pare away the wood towards the stem, so that the planking will lie snug on the surface and butt cleanly against the
outer layers of the stem piece. In this way you will get
a very neat and workman-like job. Having done this,
glue in the keel and the stem for keeps.

Your model has now got the real look of a ship, and
I expect you will want to rest from your labour and

contemplate the firstfruits thereof for a bit. This is quite a good thing to do, especially the contemplation. Look at it from every angle, stroke it all over, and really take it in, for now is the time to find out and remedy any want of symmetry or form. The under-water body of the ship is so lovely (*v.* Figs. 2 and 3) that one can spend, I will

FIG. 2.—The Model from the Fore End, showing the Under-water Body and the Headwork in early stages.

FIG. 3.—The Model from Aft, showing the Rise of Floor and the Contour of the Under-water Body. The planking of the counter can be faintly distinguished. The white line above the planking is the square landing for the knuckle moulding, and the white line on the deck level is the landing for the poop bulwark.

not say waste, hours in simply looking at it, and this quiet, ruminative inspection of your work will not only be a pleasure you are entitled to, but will add to its value, because inevitably you will discover something which you can improve.

The Forecastle Head.—The sheer line corresponds very nearly to the line of the main deck : above the main deck level are two elevations, the forecastle head and the poop. The forecastle head is decked over, and beneath it are the windlass, the cable-stoppers, and other gear, so that it cannot be made out of a solid block. Cut out a triangular piece of wood to fit into the bows : shave off the front angle in such a way that its front surface is in

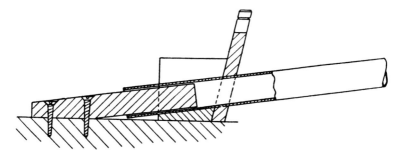

FIG. 4.—The Housing of the Bowsprit. The diagram shows the bowsprit too low in relation to the main deck. It slips through the hole in the knightheads on to the bevelled rod screwed on to the main deck.

line with the rake of the stem. The knightheads will butt up against this piece. Bore the hole for the bowsprit, which is a piece of copper tube $\frac{9}{16}$ in. in diameter. Into the after end of the bowsprit fit a short piece of wooden rod, and bevel the end so that it will lie flat on the main deck (*v.* Fig. 4). The bowsprit hole must be bored at an angle to give the correct " steve " or upward inclination. This angle must be taken off the drawing with a carpenter's bevel, using, of course, one of the horizontal lines and not the sheer line. I bored my block at what I thought was approximately the right angle, and then corrected it by planing down the base of the block until the proper angle of the steve was obtained. Put the bowsprit in

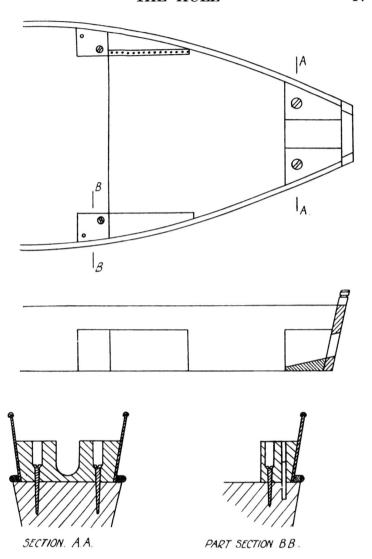

SECTION. A.A.

PART SECTION BB.

FIG. 5.—Constructional Details of the Forecastle Head Supports. The fore block is deeply grooved for the bowsprit. The after blocks form the base of the heads; under the deck the port-side block becomes the pigsty, and the starboard-side block is made to represent the paint locker.

position—having due regard to the centre line—put a couple of small screws through the bevelled rod at its after end, and then put a long thin screw through each side of the shaped block to hold it in its correct position rigidly. Set it back sufficiently to give room for the knightheads. The top of the stem piece should touch the lower side of the bowsprit for an inch outside the knightheads. The advantage of this method is that the bowsprit can be slipped in and out, and will always go back in exactly the same position. Two other blocks are needed for the forecastle head to support the after corners of the deck. They are shaped as shown in the diagram (v. Fig. 5). The part aft of the back edge of the forecastle head forms the base of the men's lavatories. The parts actually under the forecastle deck are paint lockers on the starboard side and a pigsty on the port side. The blocks should be screwed and dowelled firmly on to the main deck. Their outer surfaces are bevelled to correspond with the flare of the bows and to form a firm seating for the bulwarks. They are set back $\frac{1}{8}$ in. from the edge of the ship plus $\frac{1}{32}$ in. for the thickness of the bulwarks which will come outside them.

The three blocks must be of the same height, viz., 1 in. above the main deck, the height of the space under forecastle head being 4 ft.

Now fit an under deck upon these three blocks. It may be made of a piece of 3-ply or white sycamore, and the shape is obtained from the half-breadth plan in the drawing. Screw it down temporarily upon the blocks with $\frac{1}{4}$-in. counter-sunk screws, but before fixing it screw a cambered beam underneath it to give it a slight curvature, and mark out the centre line on its upper surface.

CHAPTER II.

DETAILS OF THE HULL

The Knightheads.—These were two stout timbers projecting upwards and forwards, and built firmly into the body of the ship on either side of the bowsprit. Their original function was to give lateral support to this spar. Like much of the headwork of a ship, the knightheads gradually disappeared. Function and ornament became inextricably mixed until, like the Life Guards of to-day, it is impossible to distinguish which is their *raison d'être*. In most of the clipper ships, however, the knightheads were not there for ornament, but performed several useful functions.

The rake at which they are set corresponds with the rake of the stem, and their forward edge is in line with the after edge of the stem piece. In section, the forward and after faces are parallel and at right angles to the centre line the ship. The inner face is parallel with the bowsprit and the outer face is bevelled to correspond with the run of the forecastle bulwark. Above and below the bowsprit the spaces between the knightheads were filled in with blocks of timber made to fit, the bowsprit being solidly bedded on the lower block. The forestay sets up to hearts bolted to the after side, and the fore topmast stay, after turning round sheaves at the fore end of the bowsprit, set up to hearts on the fore side of the knightheads. It is therefore important to have this part of the ship rigid.

I made the whole thing out of one piece of boxwood
$\frac{1}{4}$ in. thick (*v.* Fig. 6). Boring the hole for the bowsprit
requires some care. The piece of boxwood, which should
be longer than the finished knightheads, was screwed on
to a triangular-shaped block of wood fixed to the face-
plate. Owing to the angle at which the knightheads are
set and the steve of the bowsprit, it is rather a complicated
affair to set up the job for boring the hole at exactly the
right angle. The exact angle is 140°. However, by
making the sup-

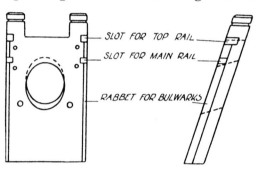

porting block the
shape of an equi-
lateral triangle and
boring the hole
slightly oversize, I
got a neat hole
and a good fit.
After boring the
hole, the sides
were planed down
and bevelled. The
ends were next
cut to the right
length, and were

FIG. 6.—The Knightheads, made in one piece,
bored out for the Bowsprit, slotted to take
the rails, and rabbeted for the bulwarks.
The small holes above the bowsprit housing
are for the forestay and fore topmast-stay
hearts, and the holes below for dowels.

bevelled so that the bottom end bedded solid on the
top of the sheer piece and the top was horizontal. To
allow it to bed down, the middle layer of the stem
piece must be cut away above the sheer piece. There
should then be a gap $\frac{1}{4}$ in. wide into which the knightheads fit, between the stem and the foreward block
which supports the forecastle deck. The top of the stem
just touches the lower edge of the hole, and if it has been
cut and fitted correctly there should be no gap between
it and the bowsprit. All this work takes a considerable
amount of time and great care to make the parts fit
properly, and it is all work with nothing to show for it

in a way. However, if the parts did not fit it would show very badly.

With the knightheads in position, mark out on their after side the level of the forecastle deck, and cut a slot into which the fore end of the covering boards will subsequently be fitted; $\frac{5}{16}$ in. above this slot cut a smaller recess, in which the end of the top rail will be housed. Then form a rabbet on the outer aspect to take the fore end of the forecastle bulwarks. This rabbet is about $\frac{1}{8}$ in. wide and as deep as the material used for the bulwarks. It runs from the bottom end as far up as the recess for the top rail. Above this recess the outer aspect is slightly hollowed out. Drill a hole on each side of the opening for the bowsprit on the fore side for the fore topmast stay hearts, and two holes on the after side for the forestay hearts. These hearts should be made and fixed in position before the knightheads are finally fixed, and if they are made with a $\frac{1}{16}$-in. screwed stalk, they can easily be screwed in.

Drill a hole also on each side below the bowsprit opening, and then, with the bowsprit in its housing and dead central, extend these holes back into the block lying behind. These holes are large enough to take small dowels, by means of which the knightheads are kept in their proper position.

Finally, the gap between the knightheads, into which the after end of the jibboom fits, is cut out, and the part is then ready to be fixed, but it is better not to fix it permanently until the forecastle deck and the covering boards have been made and fitted. The dowels and the bowsprit will keep it firmly in position while this work is being done.

Old-fashioned Headwork.—The knees of the head should be made next. These parts, again, are somewhat " vestigial," as the doctors say of the appendix, but if one understands what the parts were originally, and what

their functions were, it adds considerably to the interest
of the work. Study of a model or a good drawing of a
late eighteenth-century line of battle ship will show the
structure, but I will describe briefly those parts which
one should know about. This class of ship was very
bluff in the bows, and had a comparatively thin stem
which projected a long way forward, with the familiar
schooner bow profile. This long projection was needed
as a support for the bowsprit, which not only rested on the
stem, but was firmly lashed down to it by the gammoning.
In the old ships the bowsprit was also secured by two or
three bobstays, which were set up to the stem. All this
care to secure the bowsprit was necessary because the
foremast was set so far forward that the forestay had to
be secured to the bowsprit; and as in those days, and
indeed until about 1850, the main topmast stay set up in the
fore top, it meant that if the bowsprit were lifted from
its bed, not only would the whole foremast go but the
main topmast would lose its support as well.

It will be seen, therefore, that there was a valid reason
why the old shipwrights concentrated a good deal of their
attention upon making the stem as rigid as possible. In
order to do this they provided lateral supports which
filled up the angle between the stem and the bluff bows.
The support was given by two stout timbers, one above
the other, which fitted into the angle and extended forwards on the side of the stem and backwards on the bows
of the ship. These timbers were called the knees of the
head, or sometimes the " cheek knees." Between the
after ends of these timbers the hawse holes were situated.
The knees were set about a couple of feet apart, and the
gap between them was filled by the " trail board," which
was decorated with carving and " gingerbread " work.
The knees of the head and the trail board sweep upwards
towards the figurehead, and so help the graceful flow of
the lines of the bow. Private steam yachts are about the

only class of ship which show any trace of this work at the present day.

In addition to these parts there was also a series of head rails extending from the bows up to the figure-head. I do not know whether these rails were originally added to give any sort of structural support to the stem, but their main function in the early part of last century was to afford seating accommodation for the men when obeying the calls of Nature. In consequence, the men's lavatories in a ship were for a long time called " the heads."

Now all these parts are present in an attenuated, and I might say degenerating, form in the *Cutty Sark*. The old conservative influences in ship design still per-sisted. Shipowners were mostly individuals and not companies, and with an individual the sense of beauty and the feeling for historical continuity could still out-weigh the claims of pure utility.

The widening of the angle between the stem and the bows and the setting back of the foremast made all the difference to the headwork. As the bows became longer, sharper, and leaner, the angle increased, until from the purely practical point of view there was really no necessity for the headwork at all. However, the *Cutty Sark* had a knee on each side supporting the stem ; the outer surface of this knee representing the trail board was carved with a bevy of naked witches chasing after Nannie, the figure-head, and there was also a set of bracketed head rails on each side, and our task now is to reproduce them.

The Knees of the Head.—One solid piece of timber on each side takes the place of the two knees and trail board (*v.* Figs. 7, 8, and 9). It is not an easy piece to make, owing to the various angles and curvatures which enter into it, but if made in two halves the job becomes quite simple. First make the half which fits against the stem ; this part extends from the figurehead to the knightheads :

where it butts against the base of the figurehead it is $\frac{1}{8}$ in. from side to side and about $\frac{5}{16}$ in. vertically. The piece

PLAN OF KNEE OF HEAD

FIG. 7.—The Knee of the Head is most easily made in two pieces, joining together at the angle. The join will be covered on the outside of the trail board and below by a slip of veneer, as explained in the text.

widens as it runs aft, and also becomes deeper. When shaped, pin the port and starboard pieces together, the pins passing through the stem. Mark off on their after ends a line corresponding to the front line of the knight-

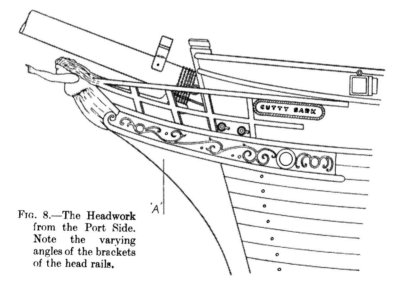

FIG. 8.—The Headwork from the Port Side. Note the varying angles of the brackets of the head rails.

heads and cut the after ends to this bevel. Now shape and fit the after half. Its fore end butts against the after end of the fore half, and is bevelled to fit. The after end widens from above downwards, but thins down to the thickness of the planking in the athwart-ship dimension. It should be quite flat against the hull, and its top edge corresponds with the sheer line.

The Hawse Hole and Pipes.—The hawse hole must be cut through this half, about an inch from its after end. The hole runs backwards, upwards, and inwards. Cut also, in the hull, a groove to be an extension of the hawse

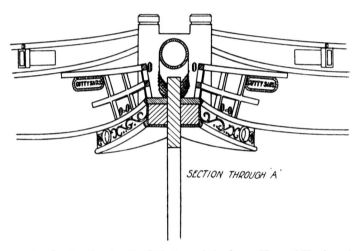

SECTION THROUGH A

Fig. 9.—Section showing the Relations of the Stem, Knee of Head, and Head Rails. The decorated part is the trail board with the hawse hole at its after end.

hole, big enough to take a copper tube of $\frac{5}{16}$ in. outside diameter. When the hawse holes are cut on both sides, insert lengths of tube; their projecting ends will show if the holes have been cut symmetrically. The hawse pipes are cut from the copper tube. The inboard end is cut to a bevel which corresponds with the level of the main deck. Carefully mark the outboard end where it passes through the knee of the head and cut it to the bevel shown by the mark. Solder the outboard end to a small piece of copper plate about $\frac{1}{16}$ in. thick, and then drill away the part of the plate that covers the bore of the tube : the hole left will be of an oval contour. Mark a line round this opening about $\frac{3}{32}$ in. external to the bore and cut away the redundant copper ; then round off both the inner and outer edges with a file. This forms the rim of the hawse pipe, which will bed solidly against the hull. The hawse pipes should be oxidised black.

After fitting the two halves of the knee to the stem and the hull, take a spokeshave and trim the outer surface, on which the trail board will subsequently be fixed, to a slight concavity. This surface need not be highly finished as it will be covered up later.

Where the two halves join below the knightheads there will be an angle projecting downwards ; pare this off with a chisel so that the under surface becomes a curve sweeping up towards the figurehead. A piece of thin veneer is cut to the shape of this surface and glued and pinned on to cover the joint.

Before continuing with the description of the headwork it will be necessary to give some attention to the stern for a time.

The Rudder Trunk.—First of all, bore the hole for the rudder trunk. The stern post slopes slightly downwards and forwards, and the hole must be bored in this direction. Now take a piece of $\frac{1}{8}$-in. 3-ply sheet, lay it on the stern, mark it round with a pencil, and cut it out to this shape. It should extend forwards as far as the break of the poop. The edge of this piece is cut square all round, and the object of it is as follows. A half-round moulding runs all round the ship. If you look at the stern of a ship you will see that this moulding separates the upper from the lower curved surfaces of the counter. This moulding is called the "knuckle." If you run the two curved surfaces directly into each other they form an angle, and it is almost impossible to fix the half-round moulding properly to form the knuckle. By putting in the flat piece with the square edge you obtain a proper landing for the half-round moulding and save yourself a lot of trouble. Screw down this piece and bore it for the rudder trunk ; being thin, it will take the very slight curvature of the sheer.

The Poop.—The raised poop is constructed next. This may be made of a solid block, as there is no gear to go underneath the deck and the saloon skylight is the only opening. It may therefore be cut out of a piece of pine an inch thick. The sides are vertical at the fore end, and gradually pass into the overhang of the counter. One of the best ways to fashion the counter is to shape it from the plank and then to cover the end grain of the wood with $\frac{1}{32}$ in. 3-ply. The pattern of the 3-ply cover can be cut out of brown paper first. It is shaped like a horseshoe. Glue this on firmly with cold-water glue, being careful to see that the 3-ply lies solid on the wood. The covering should be brought to within $1\frac{1}{2}$ in. of the forward end and cut with a clean, straight edge, so that subsequently it will fit in with the after edge of the main bulwark, and the two pieces will then lie on a solid landing.

The poop piece is bored for the rudder trunk, and can then be screwed firmly in position above the $\frac{1}{8}$-in. 3-ply. The deck is $1\frac{1}{8}$ in. above the main-deck level. On the top of the poop piece an under deck of $\frac{1}{8}$-in. 3-ply is put on, and thin slips are put underneath it, slightly curved, to give a camber to the deck. The teak deck is laid on the top of this.

In making the under deck and the overlying teak deck there is an important precaution to take. The low poop bulwark later on is glued and pinned round the vertical edge of these two layers of deck. It will be made of $\frac{1}{32}$-in. 3-ply, so that the deck must be set back all round by the thickness of the 3-ply. If this is done beforehand, it will be found quite easy later on to fit the bulwark. There will, in fact, be a proper rabbet for the bulwark to lie in (v. Fig. 10), whereas, without forming this recess, fixing the bulwark would be difficult and unsatisfactory. It is important to think of these things beforehand, and particularly in this case, since this slight bulwark has to carry a rail on the top of which the poop stanchions are fitted : it must therefore be firm and solid.

On the fore side of the poop block another covering piece of 3-ply is fitted. This is straight at the bottom and curved at the top to fit the camber of the poop deck. It is a good plan to carry the $\frac{1}{16}$-in. 3-ply under deck far enough forward to come over this front covering piece, which will then lie snugly. It is painted white.

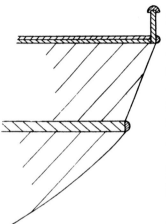

FIG. 10.—Diagrammatic Section of the Counter, to show the square landing arranged for the knuckle moulding ; on the deck level the teak deck planking and the under deck are represented, and the rabbet for the low poop bulwark.

The monkey poop, or coach-house roof, will be described later.

Another little point about the construction of the poop which should be considered is this. A shelf 6 in. wide runs all round the ship at the level of the lower half-round moulding : when it reaches the poop this shelf gradually narrows as it runs aft, until it practically disappears when it reaches the middle line, and the knuckle is formed only by the half-round moulding. The fore end of the poop block, therefore, is $\frac{1}{4}$ in. less in width than the piece of $\frac{1}{8}$-in. ply wood on which it rests, but as they run aft, the edges of the poop and the $\frac{1}{8}$-in. ply wood approach each other.

Bore the hole of the rudder trunk before screwing it down in position. If the question of weight is of any consideration, the central portion of the poop block may be sawn out, leaving the sides about half an inch thick.

Making Strip Wood.—Now cut two long pieces of wood $\frac{1}{8}$ in. square. A small circular saw which can be mounted on the lathe comes in very handy for making strip wood of various sizes. Small, very thin saws can be bought from George Adams, of High Holborn, or other tool dealers : a mandrel for them is easily and quickly made, and, personally, I have found it most convenient to be able to turn out any kind of strip, besides being much cheaper than having to buy the sections. If you have not got a saw, $\frac{1}{8}$ in. square strips can be purchased from Hobbies.

The Packing Pieces.—The $\frac{1}{8}$-in. square strip is tacked on to the top edge of the hull, flush with its outer surface : if the hull is to be planked, the strip is laid on with an allowance for the thickness of the planking. The after end of the strip butts against the edge of the $\frac{1}{8}$-in. piece of ply which lies under the poop block. Its upper surface forms the above-mentioned shelf, and the lower half-round moulding will subsequently be pinned to its outer surface. Carry the strip along to a point about 3 in. in front of the break of the forecastle and cut it off here.

It is rather difficult to describe the work in a really orderly sequence, but I may say here that the fore end of this part of the strip will be fitted against the after edge of the " bill board," and you have not got the exact position of this fixed at present.

Another length of packing strip long enough to run from the approximate position of the " bill board " to the figurehead is then tacked on to the top edge of the sheer piece outside the blocks which support the forecastle deck, and leaving space enough for the $\frac{1}{32}$-in. bulwark to be inserted between the strip and the blocks. The strip is carried along the top edge of the knees of the head and ends at the figurehead. It will be found that this piece of strip has to accommodate itself to two curves, one a concavity where it should bend in towards the foot of the knightheads, and the other where it curves upwards towards the figurehead. It may be found necessary to steam the wood to get it to take the curves easily, and in order to fix it, make a small $\frac{1}{16}$-in. screw of wire which can be screwed into the foot of the knightheads. Being made of boxwood they will hold the wire screw quite easily.

The Head Rails.—Some hours will elapse before this piece has set and dried out, which may be utilised in making the head rails, figurehead, and the name-plates, but before starting on the head rails, cut out a piece of $\frac{1}{32}$-in. 3-ply, which can be fitted temporarily in the position of the forecastle bulwark. The photograph (v. Fig. 11) shows the idea. It was taken during an early stage of the construction. From it the design of the head rails can be understood. They run from the forecastle bulwarks to the figurehead. The top rail is called the hair rail, because it runs in to the hair of the figurehead. It starts just under the cat head, and although in this photograph its top edge looks straight, it has, when properly fixed, a slight concavity.

The head rails as shown in the model are not to be seen in the actual ship. There are at present two somewhat unsightly-looking pieces of angle-iron. It is known that the present figurehead is, at any rate in part, a replacement of the original one, and the bows have sustained some damage at one time and another. It is probable that these pieces of angle-iron were built into the ship as a repair job. Rennie's sail plan shows head rails of the old-fashioned bracketed type, which gives a much more graceful look to the bows. There is plenty of evidence to show that such rails were still in use at the time the ship was built. For instance, the drawings of the *Caliph*, which was built by Hall at Aberdeen in the same year, show these bracketed head rails.

They can be made nicely of $\frac{1}{16}$-in. square boxwood

strip, with halved joints. The secret of making these
rails look right is to get the correct angles for the brackets.
They are all different, and radiate from the fore foot.
Hold a light batten to the side of the fore foot and mark
off on the rails four lines. The third is parallel with the
knightheads, the first and second are in front of them,
and the fourth behind. Glue and pin all the joints. The

FIG. 11.—The Model in an early stage of Construction. Note the main rail
running on to the forecastle, and also the angles of the brackets of the
head rails.

lower end of the brackets are halved and pinned into the
$\frac{1}{8}$-in. square packing strip. When the parts are in position,
it will be found that the brackets slope upwards and
outwards and the hair rail runs in a slightly concave course.
Pare down any upstanding edges where the brackets are
halved into the $\frac{1}{8}$-in. strip, so that the half-round moulding
which will subsequently be laid over the joints will lie
flat. The rails are painted white.

The Name-plate.—The name-plate of the ship is
attached beneath the hair rail, just in front of the cat

head. I had a die cut for a few shillings, just like the
ordinary note-paper address die, so that the name might
be embossed in raised gold letters on black paper. A piece
of thick silk thread twisted like rope was glued round the
name-plate, and when set hard the rope was gilded with
gold leaf. The name on the black paper was then cut

Fig. 12.—The Headwork on the Model. The three bull's-eyes at the break
   of the forecastle take the jibboom guys. The port back rope from the
   dolphin striker is set up to the bull's-eye just below and in front of the
   cathead, and the remaining two are for the headstays.

out to fit inside the gilded rope, and fixed with glue (v.
Fig. 12).

The Figurehead.—The figurehead, which in accordance
with custom was always painted with the best white
enamel, calls for the exercise of any talent you may possess
in carving. Various woods may be used : lime and pear
are suitable, and so is boxwood. I was given a small piece
of French walnut, which is pleasant to work and does not
split. The main thing is to get the masses right before
attempting any detailed work. Cut the block out first,

and then cut a groove in it to fit closely upon the end of the stem, so that the main axis of the figure shall flow gracefully into the lines of the bows. As a guide to the correct size, it may be noted that the extended arm is $\frac{5}{8}$ in. long. A most useful tool for this minute carving is a dental engine and a few discarded dental burrs, but some people may prefer to mould the figurehead out of one of the numerous artists' moulding materials on the market, such as Barbola.

However made, the figurehead can be quite a beautiful feature of the ship. One wants to read Burns's poem, " Tam o' Shanter," to appreciate old Willis's somewhat whimsical sense of humour in naming and decorating his ship. The figure represents Nannie, the beautiful witch, and the tale goes, that on nearing port the grey mare's tail was always put into her outstretched hand. Quite an interesting book might be written on the origin and history of figureheads. I have been told that the custom originated owing to the fact that at one time ships carried an altar dedicated to some saint in the bows, and the figure of the saint survived long after the altar disappeared. It is quite a step in evolution from the saint to Nannie (v. Fig. 13).

The original figure is said to have been an outstanding example of the wood carver's art. When every ship was ornamented with a figurehead there must have been work enough for several craftsmen, but the gingerbread work is all inside a ship nowadays, and mostly machine made at that.

The Trail Boards.—The decorative work on the trail boards is a considerable difficulty : the design of the original carving is irretrievably lost, but was said to have shocked our Victorian ancestors. The present design is a very crude bit of work. The trail boards themselves were made of $\frac{1}{32}$-in. 3-ply wood, shaped and moulded to fit the outer surface of the knee of the head. The scroll

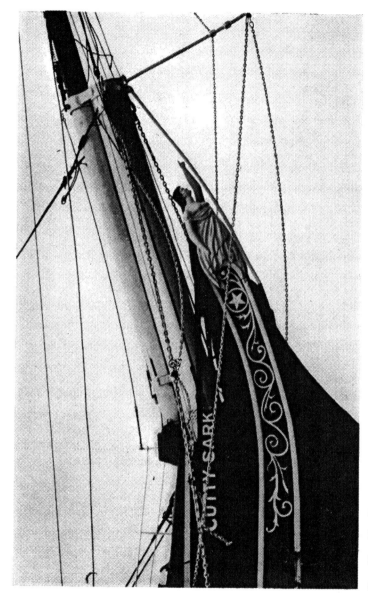

FIG. 13.—The Figurehead of the Ship. The outstretched arm is very badly modelled. The angle-iron head rails with the name-plate can be seen. This photograph is also useful for details of the jibboom, rigging, etc.

(By courtesy of the " Daily Mirror.")

work was put on as a moulding paste which was gilded when set.   A short length of half-round moulding is attached to the lower edge of the trail boards : it does not run parallel with the moulding, but diverges as it runs aft. Its forward end runs into a finial scroll carved on the side of the figurehead block.

Forecastle Port Holes.—Following the line of this piece of moulding comes a row of four port holes spaced an inch apart, which gave light to the crew's quarters under the forecastle.   If the top sides are to be planked, both the trail board and the port holes should be fixed after the planking.

The Half-round Mouldings.—The half-round moulding can be made in many different ways.   An easy way is to take a strip of wood $\frac{1}{8}$ in. thick, pare off the edges with a spokeshave and then rub it down to the desired contour with glass-paper.   When. the edge is rounded, run the strip through the saw : in this way one can get it as thick or as thin as desired.   I found an old venetian-blind slat very suitable for this, and the strips bent round the stern without any sign of splitting.

Although I have described all this part of the work together, I did not actually do the work in the sequence given.   Before fixing any of the headwork or putting on the $\frac{1}{8}$-in. square packing strip, the planking and copper sheathing were done.   These are described under separate headings.

CHAPTER III.

HOUSING THE MASTS.

A VERY important part of the work may now be undertaken, namely, the stepping of the masts. For the lower masts use copper tube, the fore and main $\frac{5}{8}$ in. and the mizzen $\frac{9}{16}$ in. in diameter. You will find that you are constantly putting in and taking out the masts during the months of construction : you can arrange that this can be done easily, and with the certainty that the masts go back in their proper position.

Importance of Rigidity of Lower Masts.—They must, of course, be dead in the centre line : they are a definite distance apart and are all set sloping backwards. This " rake " is not the same for all the masts. The rake is greatest for the mizzen and least for the fore mast. The idea of the varying rake was to allow the wind free access to the sails. A template should be cut out for each mast from the diagram given (Fig. 14), and used for determining the rake. It is a very considerable gain if you can fix your lower masts really rigidly ; when you come to put up the rigging you will appreciate the enormous advantage of having this rigidity, so take your time over this job as well. Although my directions may sound somewhat meticulous, you may be sure that your masts will be right if you follow them out.

First look at your hull : amidships, where the sheer pieces have fined away to nothing, you have the upper edge of the top plank, and you should have this upper edge available inside the sheer pieces fore and aft. This edge is, of course, horizontal and parallel with the keel, and you will need it to get a horizontal bed for the templates when you fix the rake of the masts. For each mast you want something to hold it at the bottom of the ship and another housing just below the deck.

The Upper Housing.—Start with the main mast. You will see from the drawing that the main mast is situated at station 11. At this station there are no sheer pieces. Begin by screwing on each side to the inside of the hull a shelf of $\frac{1}{4}$-in. square stuff 5 in. long ; the centre of this shelf is at station 11 and its top edge must be $\frac{1}{4}$ in. below the edge of the hull. Then take two pieces $\frac{1}{4}$ in. by $\frac{1}{2}$ in., batten and cut them so that they will lie athwartship on the shelves 3 in. apart. They must be an exact

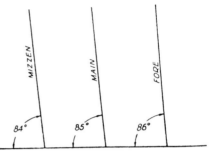

Diagram showing Rake of the Three Masts. To make templates for the rakes, extend the lines carefully · before taking off the angle.

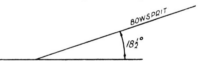

Angle of Sleve of Bowsprit.

FIG. 14.

fit. If you make them too tight they will press the sides of the hull outwards and if too loose they will be of no use. Now prepare a 3-in. square of $\frac{1}{4}$-in. stuff. Paste a piece of white paper on the top of it and pencil a line through the centre : draw another line at right angles also through the centre. Where the lines cross, drill a hole just big enough to admit the mast. This hole must be central to the lines.

Now fix a thread fore and aft along the centre line of your ship, and another thread athwartships at section 11.

Put the 3-in. square between the two battens with a touch
of glue on its fore and after edges; adjust it so that
its pencil lines correspond with the threads. When the
glue is set, take out the whole thing and screw a batten
on either side of the mast hole so that the three bits are
now rigidly fixed together. When put back on the shelf
the mast hole must always be exactly in the centre line.
The only difficulty you can meet with so far is in finding
out when the centre line thread corresponds with the
pencilled centre line on the 3-in. square, if you have already
fixed the sheer pieces, etc., because the thread will be at
a higher level. If you have this difficulty, it is quite easy
to get over it by standing a small steel square on the
pencilled line. When it touches the thread you know you
have got the right position.

If I were doing the job again I should fix the position
of the masts and their housings before putting on the sheer
pieces, then the centre-line thread would be lying directly
upon the upper housing, and it would not be necessary to
check up the lines with a square.

The Lower Housing.—Now take another piece of wood
$\frac{1}{2}$ in. thick, 2 in. wide, and long enough to rest with a little
play sideways on the bottom shelf inside the hull. This
bottom shelf is formed by the edge of the bottom plank
but one, the middle of which was sawn out earlier.
Bore a $\frac{5}{8}$-in. hole as near to the centre of this piece as you
can; it forms the lower housing of the mast. Drill also a
hole on each side to take a screw.

It now remains to get the correct rake of the mast.
Take your upper housing and gently file the edge of the
hole fore and aft so that the mast can pass through it
obliquely, judging the amount of obliquity from the rake
template. Put the mast and upper housing in position
and find the correct position of the lower housing. The
bottom of this will only touch along its after edge. Lay a
flat bit of board across the ship, not on the sheer pieces

but on the horizontal edges inside the sheer pieces, and put the horizontal edge of your template on this to test the rake of the mast. When adjusted, slip a scrap of metal or wood under the front edge of the lower housing, which is tilted up. The thickness of this bit of wood or metal tells you how much must be planed off the after edge of the under surface of the lower housing to get it to lie flat. Plane it down until by trial and error you have got it right. Then plumb the mast. I think the best way to fix the lower housings is to glue them in their respective places first : before the glue has had time to set check over the work, and be absolutely certain that the position is dead right. When the glue has set, screw the bottom housing down and the upper one to its shelf. If you put in the screws first, it is very easy in doing so to move the lower housing a very little out of place and the error would be considerably multiplied at the mast head.

It is obvious that if these housings are properly and firmly fixed (v. Fig. 15) no subsequent trouble about the position or rigidity of the masts can arise, and they can be taken out and slipped back into their correct places without any waste of time.

Once you have got the main mast fixed you can proceed to fix the fore and mizzen in the same way. The distance between the back of fore to front of main is $15\frac{1}{8}$ in., and from back of main to front of mizzen is $12\frac{5}{8}$ in. The rake of the fore is less, and that of the mizzen is more than that of the main. The three masts must, of course, be in line and vertical when looked at from the front, and form a very useful check on each other. If their upper ends are in line you can be pretty sure you are right, though a straight batten ought not to touch all three at the same time owing to the mizzen being of smaller diameter than the other two.

Before leaving this question of stepping the masts there is another point to which you might like to pay attention.

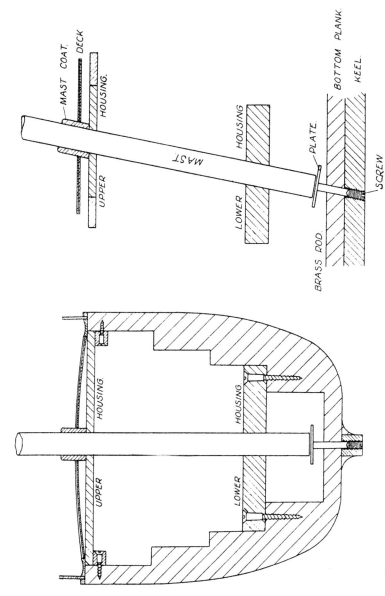

FIG. 15.—Diagram showing Method used for Housing the Masts. The plate at the foot of the mast lies on the bottom plank ; by turning the screw in the keel the mast can be raised slightly and so tighten up the rigging if necessary.

Models, especially such complicated affairs as ship models, are very delicate, and slight things such as changes of temperature, uneven shrinking of the hull, etc., may throw them out of that perfect balance in which they have left the builder's hands. One of the common things that happens is a slackening of the rigging, especially if the rigging is made of some sort of fibre, particularly cotton. A method of tightening up the rigging, therefore, is desirable, though of course this sort of thing cannot be done in any extensive manner without throwing the model out of scale. The dodge I have incorporated to tighten, or shall I say tune up, the rigging is as follows. At the foot of each mast bore a $\frac{3}{16}$-in. diameter hole through the bottom plank into the groove ploughed out for the keel. Silver solder a bit of $\frac{3}{16}$-in. round brass rod to a half-penny. Bore through the oak keel a $\frac{7}{64}$-in. hole to meet the other hole, thread it $\frac{1}{8}$ in., and insert a bit of $\frac{1}{8}$-in. screwed rod with a pointed end and a slotted top. Screw this into the keel so that it does not show. File down the $\frac{3}{16}$-in. rod so that it touches the point of the screw when the halfpenny is well down. The mast is pushed down on the halfpenny, and a whole turn of the screw will raise it $\frac{1}{40}$ in., which is quite enough to tighten the rigging. This is a dodge, however, and must not be regarded as a substitute for slack rigging, and of course it would not work at all when the rigging has slacked on one side only. If it is known beforehand that the model is likely to be constantly subjected to changes of temperature or of atmospheric humidity, it would be wise to fit a screwed brass sleeve for the screw to work in, because the thread in the oak alone would wear too quickly.

Supports.—Another point that must be considered before the work proceeds much further is the method of holding the finished model in its case. As the bottom is not flat the ordinary brass supports employed for ship models cannot be used. When the ship has a considerable

rise of floor, shaped chocks are generally fitted to form
a cradle in which the model rests. While the building is
going on such a cradle is certainly the best means of
support, but these chocks are undesirable, because they
prevent an uninterrupted view along the under-water
body of the ship. If there is anything to hide, such as a

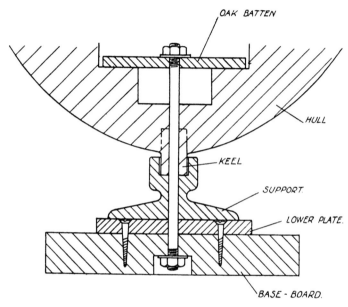

Fig. 16.—Diagrammatic Section of the Show-case Supports of the Model.
The support and lower plate are made of gun-metal.

flat or a want of symmetry, the chocks can do it, but when
the hull is as it should be, it is a pity to hide the lines in
any way. I made a pair of gun-metal supports (v. Fig. 16).
Each support was in two pieces. The upper part was a
square bar about 2 in. long slotted out to take the keel,
and was cast with a flat circular foot. The lower part
was a larger disc; four countersunk screw holes were
drilled in this with a fifth central hole to take a $\frac{3}{16}$-in.
rod. The upper part was also drilled for the rod, which

was screwed at both ends to take a nut. Holes were drilled through the bottom plank and the keel. A strip of oak $\frac{3}{8}$ in. by $\frac{3}{4}$ in. was laid on the bottom shelf inside the hull and the $\frac{3}{16}$-in. bolt passed through it, the keel, and the supports. The lower disc of the support is screwed on to the base-board of the case, and a hole is drilled large enough to take a small box-spanner to tighten up the nut on the lower end of the bolt. This arrangement holds the model quite securely, as the oak battens inside distribute the strain. If, and when, it is desired to move the model from place to place, temporary chocks should be placed in position fore and aft. Broad wedges are then inserted between the arms of the chocks and the hull to give additional support and to prevent the hull from swinging from side to side as it would do if held only by the bolts passing through the keel. Tissue paper backed by some fabric packing should be placed between the wedges and the hull to prevent any damage to the latter. When wedged up in this way the model can travel in its glass case with comparative safety.

THE RUDDER.

Shape of the Rudder.—The shape of the rudder and its size can be taken off the drawing. The fore edge is rounded, and it thins down towards the after edge, which is also rounded. The shaft or stock can be spliced on to the body and is in the same straight line as the fore edge. The stock is $\frac{3}{16}$ in. in diameter. In order to turn, the axis of rotation must be in the centre of the stock.

The Gudgeons and Pintles.—The rudder is attached by means of four gudgeons and pintles (v. Fig. 17). The gudgeons are eyes attached by means of straps to the stern post. The pintles are pins which are attached to the rudder. The centres of the eyes and the pins must

all lie in the same axis as the centre of the rudder stock.
If they are out of line the rudder will bind.

The gudgeons are made of short lengths of $\frac{3}{32}$-in.
copper tube soldered to the centre of a piece of $\frac{1}{16}$-in.

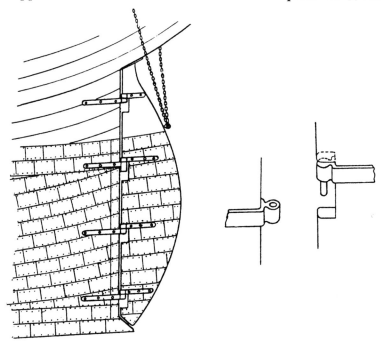

Fig. 17.—The Rudder is Hung by Four Pintles to Four Gudgeons strapped
on to the Stern. The gaps under the gudgeons allow the pintles to be
lifted when unshipping the rudder. Under the second gudgeon there is
a special bearing which takes most of the weight of the rudder, and so
prevents undue wear on the other three. The chains take no weight,
but may be used to move the rudder if the stock should happen to get
damaged. Small drawing shows a gudgeon and a pintle.

brass strip. Before soldering the two pieces together
bend the strips to fit the stern post, and be sure to solder on
the tube centrally. Three holes are bored in each strap
for nailing it on. The pintles are made in the same way,
except that a short piece of wire is soldered into the tube.
File it down when fixed so that just under $\frac{3}{32}$ in. projects.

The straps for the first and fourth pintles are short owing to the shape of the rudder.

Having made the pintles and gudgeons, cut out from the fore edge of the rudder square gaps $\frac{3}{16}$ in. vertically and horizontally. The gap must be wide enough for both pintle and gudgeon to lie in it, one above the other, without touching. If ever the rudder had to be taken off it was disengaged by jacking up the rudder. The pintles then came up out of their respective gudgeons and the rudder could be drawn. The rudder trunk, or hollow tube in which the rudder stock lies as it goes up through the counter, is made big enough to allow a slight tilt.

In fixing the pintles the most important thing is to have them all in line and in the central axis of the stock, and they must be hard up against the top edge of the gap.

The pintles and gudgeons were generally made of gun-metal in order to avoid as far as possible any galvanic action taking place with the copper sheathing. As the weight of the rudder was considerable—although being made of timber it has a tendency to float—an appreciable amount of wear took place. To minimise this wear it was arranged that the main weight of the rudder should rest on the second or the third pintle, which was made a little longer than the other three. A special bearing was fixed under the second or third gudgeon, and the pintle rested on this bearing. The other three pintles were thus lifted very slightly off their gudgeons, and while retaining their full efficiency in respect of their hinge function, they were relieved of all weight.

It will be seen from the diagram that when the rudder is shipped in position there is a space under the gudgeons. It was possible that the rudder might float up and disengage. To prevent an accident of this nature a wooden block was sometimes fitted in the gap under one of the gudgeons ; it was fixed to the rudder by a yellow metal bolt which could be knocked out at any time if it were necessary to unship the rudder.

An eye bolt is fitted to the after edge, just above the copper, to which the emergency steering chains were shackled. The steering gear occasionally broke down, and fractures of the rudder stock were not unknown. In the former case the ship was steered by tackles hooked into eye bolts on the after end of the emergency tiller on deck. If, however, the rudder stock were broken, the only method available for steering the ship was by means of these chains shackled to the eye bolt above mentioned. The rudder trunk is a copper tube with an eccentric flange soldered to its lower end, and made to fit the surface of the counter. It is kept in position by a pin through its forward side.

CHAPTER IV.

PLANKING THE HULL.

The Reason for Planking the Hull.—The effect of planking and copper sheathing the hull is so excellent in giving a real ship-like appearance to the model that it is well worth the time and trouble they take. I anticipated, and met with, difficulty about planking the stern and in setting out the goring of the copper sheathing, but I will explain and, I hope, remove these difficulties for anyone who is keen enough to want to produce the effect. The planking is an effect only, in that it is sham planking, and is only a veneer laid on in strips. Personally, I should very much like to see a real scale model of a composite ship built by an expert, but I am afraid it would be almost too difficult a job for an amateur to undertake. Although I am ready to confess that the hull planking in my model is a sham, yet it is a sham that can be defended in that it gives the external appearance of the real thing in a way which could not be obtained by any other method short of going the whole hog and building a planked model on iron frames.

The Material.—The material used for the planking was $\frac{1}{32}$-in. 3-ply. This is very useful material for model purposes and most amenable in adapting itself to any reasonable curves and twists imposed upon it. It can be obtained in sheets about a yard square, and is quite cheap, and stocked by any up-to-date cabinetmaker. The disadvantage of using it is that, if you get any high spots and want to scrape or rub down your work, you can very easily rub through the top layer. The next time I do a similar job I shall use, I think, a fine-grained wood, such as French walnut, and saw it into $\frac{1}{32}$-in. planks.

Cutting the Planks.—However, I will describe the method I used. Lay the sheet on a flat board, lay a metal straightedge upon it, and cut it up into strips $\frac{1}{4}$ in. wide with a sharp-pointed knife. However sharp the knife is the edges are bound to be a bit ragged, and must be planed. The top-side planking of the *Cutty Sark* is 11 in. wide, so the $\frac{1}{4}$-in. strips by the time the edges have been planed down will represent 11 in. There is an easy dodge for planing down these edges. Nail a couple of pieces of $\frac{1}{4}$-in. by $\frac{1}{2}$-in. strip wood on to a flat board with a gap of about $\frac{1}{2}$ in. between them, and punch in the nail heads. Take as many of the $\frac{1}{4}$-in. strips as will make a tight fit, edges upwards, in the gap between the two bits of strip wood, and see that they are all touching the bottom of the gap. A stop at the end will prevent them from sliding out. Skim them over with the plane. Take them out and turn them over, and skim over the other edge and you will have clean-edged strips just under $\frac{1}{4}$ in. wide.

For the planking of the bows you will want some strips which gradually fine down from $\frac{1}{4}$ to $\frac{3}{16}$ in. wide. Cut some $\frac{1}{4}$-in. strips as before and plane both edges. Now, for the sake of your plane, see that the nails holding down the guide strips are well punched in, and then plane them down so that about 18 in. towards the stop end thin down from $\frac{1}{4}$ to $\frac{3}{16}$ in. at the stop. Insert the 3-ply strips again and plane them to this guide.

Fairing the Strakes.—Having cut sufficient planks you are now ready to start. The whole beauty of the work consists in getting an even run on the strakes of planking from bows to stern ; the strakes must be fair and symmetrical on both sides of the ship. By far the most difficult part is underneath the counter and round the rudder trunk. There are curves in three dimensions here to be negotiated by one or, at most, two planks. It is that curved corner between the counter and the vertical part of the stern which is the greatest teaser. In steel shipbuilding there is a special plate in this position, known as the oxter plate, and it is by far the most difficult plate for the shipwright to fashion ; it is just one of those few remaining instances of a job which can still be better done by a craftsman than by a machine. Indeed I believe that no machine in existence can fashion a proper oxter plate, and I have noticed that in many of the post-war steamers I have looked at there is no true oxter plate at all, but the plates are wangled in an angular way which deprives the stern of its full complement of fascinating curves.

Planking the Counter.—As the stern is the difficult part, you must start here ; when you have surmounted the difficulty you can enjoy doing the rest of the work, which you could not do if you still had the difficult part ahead. The basic fact is that the planks meet in a mitre in the centre line between the rudder hole and the top of the counter. Three planks and half another plank meet at this mitre (*v.* Fig. 18). For setting out the angle of the mitre it will simplify matters to have an idea of the number of planks involved. There are twelve strakes visible at the bow, six amidships, and fifteen at the stern. One need hardly be so meticulously accurate as to stick entirely to these numbers, but they help in setting out the planking. No. 12 plank is the one actually pierced for the rudder hole. Make this one a little wider than the others, since it has to curve a little in the direction of its width. Cut it about 6 to 8 in. long. You must find the correct run of this plank first of all, and in order to do so proceed as follows. Take half a dozen of the $\frac{1}{4}$-in. strips and tack them on to the hull amidships edge to edge. Now press the top strip to the surface of the hull and follow it along towards the stern, keeping it flat on the surface. You will find that, whereas amidships it lies vertically, as it runs aft it gradually twists

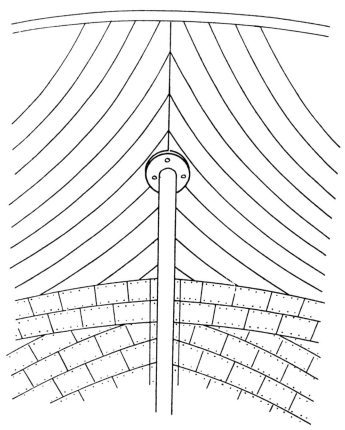

Fig. 18.—Layout of Planking at the Stern: the planks are mitred on the centre line.

so that its inner surface tends to face upwards, and some way along the counter it comes away from the hull altogether. Let it follow its natural twist, and tack it in this position. Do the same with the others, the great point being that they shall lie flat on the surface of the hull. Keep their edges hard up against each other as far as you can consistently with their lying flat. Now you will find that under the counter it is impossible to make them all lie flat and at the same time keep their edges together, the reason being that the surface of the counter is expanded, and to cover it neatly the planks will have to be cut slightly wedge-shaped, like the leaves of a fan. Leave this till later, but realising this, get your sixth plank to lie in a fair and natural run. It ought to run off the counter with its inner surface facing upwards about 1 in. forward from the centre line of the counter.

Setting Out the Strakes.—Proceed to set out on the counter the subsequent strakes in the same way, tacking them temporarily in position ; you will in this way obtain the fair line for the twelfth plank. Remember that only about 6 or 7 in. of the length of this plank will show, as its forward end runs down under the water-line and the copper. It is obviously necessary to get this fair line for setting the plank, because although you might perhaps guess at it, the odds are that you will guess wrong, and the error would show all through the planking and spoil the job, so it is the quickest way in the long run to set it out properly. Turn the ship upside down and mark on the hull with a sharp scriber the centre line, between the rudder hole and the top of the counter.

Lay your No. 12 plank to the fair line and cut the mitre to the centre line : with a small gouge cut out of the plank half the rudder hole, leaving a very small shoulder of the plank at the fore end of the hole. Cut the opposite plank to match.

The Rudder Trunk.—A dummy stern post is now needed. Take a strip of boxwood about $\frac{1}{32}$ in. thick and cut it to the shape shown in the diagram (v. Fig. 19). The tiny shoulder will press up against the plank and keep it in position. Make also a rudder trunk out of a bit of thin copper tube $\frac{1}{4}$ in. outside diameter. Push this through the rudder hole and mark it off so that when cut diagonally it will lie flush with the run of the counter. File it to an exact fit with the line of the counter. Take a small bit of copper 'sheet and drill a $\frac{3}{64}$-in. hole in it. Twist a bit of copper wire round a bit of scrap ; thread the ends through the hole and then through the tube. Twist the wire round another bit of scrap so that the bevelled end of the tube is pressed tightly on the copper sheet, and silver solder the two together. Then drill through the sheet and file the sharp edges off the oval hole obtained : cut away the sheet to leave a small circular flange, *not* concentric with the tube.

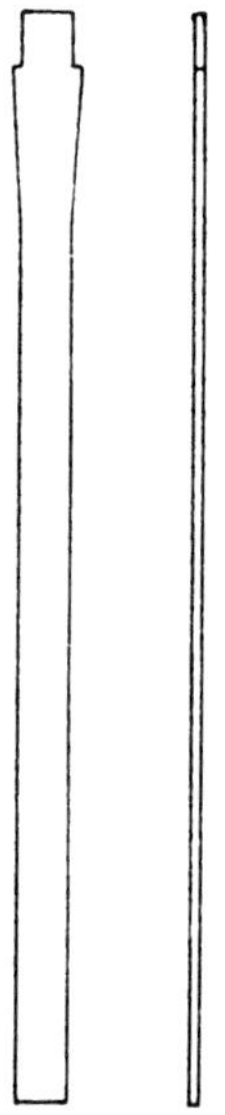

Fixing the First Plank.—Having prepared these two accessories, glue down the two No. 12 planks in position, seeing that they make a neat joint at the mitre. Push up the dummy stern post so that its shoulders press up the plank : insert the rudder tube, pushing it up so that its flange shall squeeze the plank hard up against the hull. Fix the tube with a clamp above so that it will continue to exert pressure while the glue is setting.

FIG. 19.—Dummy Stern Post. The shoulder at the upper end holds the first plank, laid close up to the rudder trunk.

I have entered into perhaps an unduly long description about this twelfth plank, as I found it much the most difficult, but I hope this explanation of the method I employed may be of use to others.

Having No. 12 fixed, Nos. 11, 10, and 9 are fairly easy, the points to watch being the mitre on the centre line and keeping the run of the planks fair.

No. 13 is also a bit tricky. Cut it about 3 in. long. Its after end must widen out and its upper edge must be slightly concave, running up to a point at its upper and after angle. Pare away the wood of the hull in front of the dummy stern post so that a rabbet is formed and the after edge of the plank lies clean up against the dummy stern post. The photograph of the model (Fig. 3) shows the run of the planking on the counter.

The lower planks will be found to fit quite easily and need no special mention.

You may now congratulate yourself on having accomplished the only difficult part of the job, and carry on with the easy part.

Planking of the Bows.—The bows have already got a rabbet ready to receive the ends of the planks ; use the tapered planks with the $\frac{3}{16}$-in. end in the rabbet. Tack them in position first, watching that they run symmetrically on the two sides ; they will want a line of tacks about 3 in. and again about 6 in. aft of the stem to hold them snug against the curvature of the bows. Cut off the ends at different lengths, so that the butts do not all come in the same line.

From the bows run the strakes to meet the ends of the after planks in fair lines. There is no difficulty at all in this part of the work and I need not describe it. When you come to fixing the planks permanently use cold-water glue : it has less tendency to make the wood swell, and it is extraordinarily tenacious ; its disadvantage being that it stains wood dark, but as the hull will be coloured black later on this will not matter.

Trimming the Planks.—There is just a point to be careful about when you come to trim the planks which cover the counter. Do not take a spokeshave and trim them with the cutting blade vertical, but lay a sharp plane on the top of the poop and shave them off with a horizontal cut. You will be surprised how far they extend beyond the original hull. Strictly speaking, in a scale model one ought to allow for this planking, because it adds $\frac{1}{16}$ in. to

the beam and nearly $\frac{1}{8}$ in. to the length. I confess, however, that I did not do so.

Pinning the Planking.—The planking should now be
pinned to the hull by tiny dowels. In the real ship the
planking is bolted on to the iron frames and the countersunk bolt holes are filled with teak dowels in the same
way that a deck is fastened. The glue will hold the planking securely, but in order to make it doubly secure dowels
may be used as well, and will show up on a very close
inspection of the work. For the method of making minute
dowel rods, see the section on Laying the Deck. The only
remaining part of this work is the scraping and rubbing
down. Very little of either will be needed : one wants
to avoid as much as possible filling up the fine line which
divides the planks ; dust from sand-papering tends to do
this and should be gently brushed out afterwards. I
thought of running a fine graver along the joints so that
the lines would show up better, but decided against doing
it because the general effect of planking is there all right.

CHAPTER V.

COPPER SHEATHING.

The Ship Worm.—Before the days of iron and steel ship-building one of the greatest enemies which wooden ships encountered was the teredo or ship worm. The animal grows to a length of 6 to 8 in., and is about as thick as the little finger. It will eat its way into any wood, teak included, and leaves its empty track behind. A curious fact about these tracks is that they never run into each other. Most museums have a bit of old worm-eaten ship timber in their show-cases, and when one looks at these specimens one wonders how an infected ship managed to hold together. All sorts of devices were tried to circumvent the attacks of the worm. The old East Indiamen used to have their bottoms thickly studded with iron nails : naval ships were at one time coated with a mixture of tallow, tar, and sulphur beneath an outer skin of wood. Lead was also tried, but before the principles of galvanic action were understood ; it was put on with copper nails and naturally soon fell off. Copper sheathing was also a failure at first, because it was put on with iron nails, but when copper nails were used it was an immediate success.

Copper when properly applied not only prevents absolutely the attacks of the teredo, but, owing to a slight chemical action which takes place with sea-water, a compound is formed which is poisonous to barnacles, although weeds can grow.

Size of the Plates.—A layer of tarred felt about $\frac{1}{4}$ in.

55

thick was generally laid under the copper. The metal was rolled in sheets 4 ft. long by 15 in. wide, the weight varying from 22 to 28 oz. per square foot. The heavier sheet was generally used at the bows and along the keel. Large copper tacks about 1½ in. long were employed to fix the sheets.

Overlap of the Plates.—They were laid in a regular fashion with the after edge of the front plate overlapping the fore edge of the after plate, 1 in. overlap being allowed. As regards the overlap of the strakes, there were two methods. In the navy, the upper edge of the lower plate overlapped the lower edge of the upper plate. In merchant ships, on the other hand, the lower edge of the upper plate overlapped the upper edge of the lower plate. There was really no advantage in one method over the other. The vertical joint, of course, comes in the centre of the plate above and below, like the slates on a roof.

In setting out the strakes of the sheathing due regard was paid to economy, and the plates were cut with a view to as little wastage as possible. As a matter of fact, the work can be done with practically no waste at all, because the pieces cut off a plate will generally fit in elsewhere.

In sheathing a model it is essential that the strakes should run in fair lines, otherwise the sheathing will look all wrong and the model would look better without it. It must be symmetrical, also, so that when looked at from either end the top edge of the copper on the two sides is at the same level.

Setting Out the Strakes.—Face up to the problem of setting out the strakes to start with. The surface of a ship's hull is a complicated system of curves of all sorts running into each other, which you have to cover in some more or less geometrical pattern of straight lines. Set your model up on an even keel on a level table and mark off all round it a horizontal line just above the level of the water-line. The copper was usually put on 6 in. above the load-line.

With a strip of paper measure (1) stem from keel to this horizontal line, (2) stern ditto, (3) amidships ditto. You must use something flexible to take these measurements, as amidships it is the extent of the curved surface you want to know and a pair of callipers will not give you this correctly. Say the amidships measurement amounts to 9 in., that would mean that 36 strakes $\frac{1}{4}$ in. wide would be needed to cover it. The stem or stern measurement may be 5 in., equal to 20 strakes. The problem is how to expand the 20 strakes at the bow into 36 amidships and then contract the latter down again to 20 at the stern in such a way that no " stealers " come in and the strakes are fair in line. It is done by what is called " goring." I had a photograph taken of my model with cotton threads fixed along the lines of the " goring," which shows the general idea (v. Fig. 20).

Material.—The material to use is copper-shim $\frac{3}{1000}$ in. thick, hard rolled. This can be bought cheaply ; it varies, of course, with the price of copper, but as far as I remember I think I paid about threepence a foot for it from Stanton Brothers, Metal Merchants, Shoe Lane, Holborn Circus. It is in strips 6 in. wide, and I used about 4 or 5 yds. of it.

The metal must be cut into plates 1 in. long and $\frac{5}{16}$ in. wide. A machine would make short work of this part of the job, but few amateurs possess the appropriate machine and it has to be done by hand. Each plate must be a right-angled rectangle, and they must all be of exactly the same size. Moreover, they must be flat, and the edges should not show any trace of curl. If you cut this thin shim with a pair of scissors one edge of the cut always tends to curl.

After some experimenting and cogitating I hit on a method of cutting the plates which is simple, accurate, and quick. One generally finds that the simpler a method of doing anything is, the better are the results, so I will describe exactly the method I used.

Cutting the Plates.—I have a piece of plate glass about 2 ft. by 1 ft. which I use as a surface plate for marking out.

Lay a piece of plate glass about this size on a firm table and put the roll of shim on it, unrolled, with its concavity down. You must be gentle with shim as it is

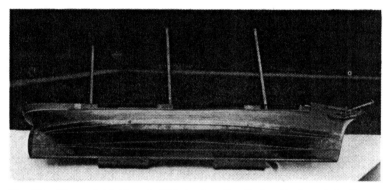

FIG. 20.—The model laid on its Side to show the Goring Strakes of the Copper Sheathing. The white lines are cotton threads. There are five zones in the sheathing: (1) The horizontal water-line belt; (2) the upper goring strakes; (3) the central horizontal belt; (4) the lower goring strakes; (5) the lower or keel horizontal belt.

very easy to kink it and very difficult, if not impossible, to eradicate the marks of ill-treatment. First, square up the end. Lay a flat steel ruler—any straight-edged bit of stock will do—on the shim, put a square on it, and cut it. Now, as regards cutting: it sounds rather Irish, but I did my cutting without cutting at all. With the point of an old scalpel, which had seen other service, I ran down the line of the steel ruler, pressing firmly on the ruler with the left hand to prevent it from slipping, and also on the knife. The point of the latter has the hard, smooth surface of the glass beneath it. Do not run over the cut twice.

Keep the ruler in place; slip the point of the knife between the copper and the glass, just to turn it up. Then with the handle of the scalpel turn the copper up along the edge of the ruler to a right angle. Press it down flat again. Turn it up once more, and it will come off in a clean break along the line of the mark.

Marking off the Plates.—Having squared the end of the material, mark it off vertically in inches at the end. About 18 in. from the end mark it off again, being careful that the inch marks are vertical to the edge of the material. Now with the knife as before, mark lines between the inch marks, so that the 18 in. of material is marked by five parallel lines an inch apart. You will see the object of these lines in a moment.

A gauge of $\frac{5}{16}$-in. square stuff is needed. It should be exactly square in section and 7 or 8 in. long. Another useful adjunct is a piece of flat stuff, steel or glass, which will lie dead flat on the plate glass. This is to act as a stop for the edge of the shim to butt against. I used the blade of a Stanley square.

Put the stop on the glass; push the squared edge of the shim against the stop; put the $\frac{5}{16}$-in. gauge on the copper and push the steel ruler up against the gauge. You will quickly acquire the habit of holding the stop, gauge, and ruler together, and detect the slightest slip of the copper underneath them. It certainly does tend to slip about a little on the polished glass. Hold the ruler down firmly with the left hand, take out the gauge, mark the copper with the knife as already described, and break off the resulting strip. With a minimum of practice you will soon be able to do this without leaving the slightest curl on the edge. This strip is 6 in. long and $\frac{5}{16}$ in. wide, and has knife-marks spaced an inch apart running at right angles across it. When these are broken through, there remain six rectangular plates an inch long and $\frac{5}{16}$ in. wide. It is not exactly an exhilarating pastime to cut up about a couple of thousand of these little plates : it is better to make a few hundred at a time, so that one's fingers holding down the ruler do not have time to get tired. Every now and then put on the square, to make sure that the cut is not getting off the right angle. This method of cutting them is quick, and if properly carried out extremely accurate ; the plates are all right-angled and have no annoying curls at the angles and edges.

The Keel Plates.—A certain number of plates must be $\frac{1}{2}$ in. wide to cover the keel, and these are bent at a right angle in the direction of the length, leaving a flange of $\frac{5}{32}$ in. which lies on the bottom of the keel.

The Rivets.—The nails used for fixing the sheets were minute copper nails $\frac{3}{16}$ in. long and about $\frac{1}{32}$ in. diameter. They can be obtained in twopenny packets containing about a thousand from the Craftworkers' Supply Association, 90 Wardour Street. They also make excellent rivets. You will want about ten or twelve thousand. The easiest way to use these nails is to turn a hundred or so into the lid of a cardboard box, tilt it, and give it a gentle shake and all the heads will lie one way. Many of these little nails, which are evidently pressed out, have tiny flanges adhering to the point ; perhaps you may be able to persuade some one to snip these off for you. To handle these nails you must have a pair of forceps ; catch hold of them by the head, push them in, and give a little twist before letting go. Sweep the floor after a day's work at this plating, if you are of an economical frame of mind.

The Tools Required.—The tools needed are a small jeweller's hammer with a ball pane and flat head, a pair of cutting nippers, and a fairly stout round needle in a handle ; in addition, a few long thin battens of $\frac{1}{32}$-in. 3-ply, such as you used for planking the top sides.

When all these preparations are complete you are ready to begin the job.

Plating the Keel.—Have the hull lying upside down

and nail the bent plates on the keel with the $\frac{5}{32}$-in. flange on the bottom. The flanges of the two sides will just meet. Lap the front over the back plate. The keel is rather a discouraging part to start on, because the tiny nails have some difficulty in penetrating the hard oak. Hold a plate in position and push the needle through it, making a hole in the wood beneath : the burr formed on the under side of the metal tends to hold it in position. Put a nail in the hole and knock it in, but not right in. Snip off the head with the nippers and rivet the nail down with the ball pane, the object being to spread the cut end of the nail just enough to prevent it from slipping right through the plate. You will have plenty of practice at this, and the bottom of the keel, where it will not show, is the best place to begin practising. In general, you should allow just under $\frac{1}{16}$ in. overlap of the plates, and the nails at the overlap go through both plates.

When sheathing the keel remember to cut holes in the copper where the brass screws for regulating the rigging tension lie in the keel, and where the bolts of the gun-metal supports come.

The upper edge of the keel plates will come a shade above the line where the keel joins what would be the garboard strake in a built-up ship. The garboard strake is the strake which lies next to the keel. It was always very thick and strong.

The Lower Parallel Belt.—Eight parallel strakes are now put on, joining on to the keel plates. These eight strakes will amount to about 2 in. or a little more in width. At the stem and the stern they will be vertical, but amidships they will lie nearly horizontal. Take a strip of paper 4 ft. long and 2 in. wide. Hold it with the ends vertical on a table, then get some one to press down the middle sideways : that will be the shape of the first eight strakes.

Fairing the Strakes.—In order to keep the strakes fair, tack a batten with its lower edge $\frac{1}{4}$ in. above the top of

the keel strake and lay the plates up to the batten, which
is, of course, taken off when the strake is laid. Lay two
strakes alternately on each side of the ship, checking the
lines frequently to see that you are keeping them symmetrical until you have completed the eight strakes on
each side. You will get on quicker and drop fewer nails
as you proceed.

Setting Out the Central Belt.—A central parallel belt of
about ten strakes is laid later and must now be set out.
Mark a point on the stem $2\frac{1}{2}$ in. above the copper you
have already put on and another point at the same height
on the stern post. Stretch between these points a length
of narrow tape ; the run of the tape must be fair and
correspond more or less with the sheer of the ship. It
will therefore show a concavity upwards. To get the
parallel line for the lower edge of this belt use a strip of
paper $2\frac{1}{2}$ in. long. Measure from the lower edge of the
tape with the strip, and prick a mark where the other end
comes. Do this at intervals of about 4 in. along the tape.
Now tack on a batten with its lower edge touching the
marks you have pricked. This batten when fixed will
show a concavity downwards, and yet it is parallel with
the tape, which is concave upwards. I wasted hours
trying to set out this parallel belt with long strips of paper
which would not fit anyhow, until I tumbled to this method
of setting it out.

The Lower Goring Strakes.—You are now ready to
continue the sheathing. You do not begin on the central
belt yet, but must fill in the gap between the belt already
laid and the batten with the " goring strakes." These
strakes will be parallel with those already laid, but when
you come near the ends you will find that the plates have
to be cut to fit up to the batten. These cut plates form
what are called the " gores " : it will take about six
strakes with gored ends to fill up the space between the
horizontal lower belt and the batten. Lay these goring

strakes on both sides of the ship, checking off the run of the batten on each side for symmetry.

The Central Belt.—Now lay the lowest strake of the main parallel belt. This strake will cover all the pointed ends of the gores ; by the time you have finished the main belt the work will be taking on a very pleasing appearance.

The Upper Parallel Belt.—The water-line should now be scribed again all round the ship. A parallel belt of two or more plates wide is laid along this, $\frac{1}{8}$ in. above it to be correct, leaving a gap between it and the main belt. This gap is also filled in with goring strakes.

Before you can start on these latter goring strakes there is another little matter which requires attention. The ends of the planking strakes at the bow and stern run down to the copper, and if the copper plates were nailed direct on to them some irregularity would result. Cut off the redundant ends of the planks and carefully rub them down so that they fade away into the surface of the hull ; if necessary, fill in with a little plastic wood to get a smooth and fair bed for the copper.

The Upper Goring Strakes.—This done, lay the upper goring strakes ; two or three will be needed—it depends on how much concavity you gave to the tape. Then finish with the two or more parallel strakes, with the upper edge $\frac{1}{8}$ in. above the water-line.

Fairing the Water-line Strake.—A word of warning is necessary here. If you lay the strakes on the scribed water-line along its whole length something will look wrong. You will find that to the eye the line sags at the bows and stern, although it is truly horizontal. This is an optical effect, due to the curvature of the surface, and to circumvent it you must raise the line very slightly, $\frac{1}{4}$ in. is ample, at the bows and the stern.

Plating the Stem and Stern Posts.—The only remaining point to notice is the treatment of the plates at the bows and stern.   At the bows, turn the plates over the angle of the stem and cut them up the middle line.   They are then covered by the flat beading which is fixed to the front of the stem from the keel up.   The stern post should be covered with three-sided bent plates, the forward ends

Fig. 21.—The Model from Aft.   Note the upper goring strakes of the sheathing running under the upper horizontal belt.   The midship and quarter bumpkins are swung out.   The small davit aft is for the accommodation ladder.   Note also the supports on the keel.

of which run underneath the after edges of the plates in front of them.   The rudder should also be sheathed up to the water-line.

Undoubtedly it is a long job : it took me about 200 hours, I think, but I was at first very uncertain how to proceed.   The result is, however, satisfactory, and really does show how this type of ship was sheathed, and is therefore of some permanent instructional value.   No particular skill is required, and anyone following the directions I have given can attain the same result if content to exercise the necessary patience.

Colouring the Copper.—After a sheathed ship has been in sea-water for a little time the copper turns colour, the prevailing tint being green. It does not discolour uniformly like a copper-covered roof. I asked all sorts of people about methods of turning the copper green and experimented with all sorts of mixtures. I thought at one time that a daily wash with sea-water was going to do the trick. Finally, I painted it over with a solution of sal ammoniac and allowed it to dry on. The copper will go green under this treatment, but leaves a powdery deposit which has to be brushed off. The strength of the solution was 1 oz. to a pint of water. The chemical action is slightly corrosive, and therefore it is unwise to apply too much of it to such thin copper. The discoloration is bound to be a little irregular if the copper is not absolutely clean : it is advisable to wipe it over with a little spirit before applying the sal ammoniac. At the same time, it must be remembered that the natural discoloration of the copper was somewhat patchy, and a too uniform effect should therefore not be aimed at (*v.* Fig. 21).

Men who have served their time as apprentices in sailing ships have told me that if the mate could find nothing else for them to do while lying in harbour, they were sent over the side to polish up the top strakes of the copper. The top strake or two can therefore be left in its natural state.

CHAPTER VI.

THE DECK.

Lining a Deck.—To look shipshape the deck should be properly " laid," that is, made up of separate planks as in the real ship. More work is needed, but the result justifies the trouble taken. The alternative plan is to make the deck of one sheet and then to draw lines with a drawing-pen to represent the joints between the planks. This is not so easy as it sounds. Before drawing the lines it is essential to size the wood well, otherwise the ink will run. Black indian ink should be used. Personally, I have not succeeded in drawing these fine parallel lines satisfactorily for a long stretch of deck. The plan works well for the comparatively short, broken-up decks of steamships, but for the long sweep of main deck, as found in a sailing ship, a laid deck is, I think, easier to turn out satisfactorily, and it does represent in miniature the real thing.

Deck planking is laid according to a very definite scheme. It is not like the flooring of a house, where the boards are nailed down anyhow, so long as the ends or butts of the boards meet on a joist. So that the model builder, even if he elects to line his deck with a pen, may read this section with advantage if he does not already know how the work is carried out.

Design of Deck Planking.—If one studies a deck, the first thing that one notices is that the butts of the planks run in parallel lines across the deck, and that there are

66

generally four planks between any two butts athwartships. This is called a four-step butt deck. Occasionally there are three planks, but four is the more usual number. The planks are, of course, all of the same width, and as far as possible of the same length. The teak logs as supplied to the shipyard are not always of the same length, but the skilful shipwright will lay out a deck with the minimum of cutting and wastage, using 18, 19, 20, or 21 ft. planks. If he has to work with planks of varying lengths, the fore and aft distance between all the butts will not be quite the same, but he will always work his deck so as to bring the butts in parallel lines athwartships. I believe there is a Board of Trade rule which lays down that the minimum distance fore and aft between butts on a main deck shall be 3 ft. 6 in.

However, for model work the planks can all be cut of the same length, and therefore we need not be bothered with the complication of using planks of varying lengths. When planks of the same width and length are used, the butts will run, not only in parallel lines athwartships, but also in diagonal parallels. A glance at the diagram will show this. There is a very definite pattern, and the underlying idea of it is to separate the butt joints as far from each other as possible, and thus to aid the strength and rigidity of the deck.

Dowelling of Decks.—Close inspection of deck planking will reveal the presence of a series of round plugs let into the planks. These dowels in a steamer's deck cover up the heads of the bolts which hold the wooden deck on to the steel deck plating underneath, and, when the deck is fully plated, are placed without any reference to the deck beams which carry the steel deck. In a composite vessel there was no iron or steel deck plating on the top of the deck beams, so the wooden deck was bolted directly on to the beams, and the bolt holes were filled with the dowels; each plank, therefore, had a dowel in the centre of its width wherever it crossed a deck beam, and one close to each end to secure the butt from rising.

The diagram (Fig. 22) will, I hope, make this explanation plain, but for the sake of clearness only the dowels at the butts are shown. The foregoing remarks apply to the straightforward part of the work, but there are modifications to be made where the straight fore and aft planking meets the curves towards the bows and the stern.

The Waterways.—It will be remembered that a strip of $\frac{1}{8}$-in. square material was tacked along the top edge of the hull. The deck itself does not occupy the whole of

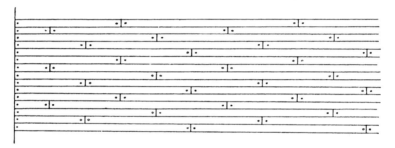

FIG. 22.—Diagram of Planking of a Four-step Butt Deck.

the space between these strips. Just inside the bulwarks are found the "waterways." In the *Cutty Sark* they are 21 in. wide, and therefore $\frac{7}{16}$ in. in the model. They are not flat, but curved, with the concavity upwards to form a wide gutter for the water constantly filling the deck in bad weather. The gutter is formed in cement, and is grey in colour at present. Many ships had their waterways painted red, and this was one of the conservative ideas inherited from fighting days when the scuppers ran red. The inboard surface of the gun ports of the *Victory* are painted red also, and I am told that the camouflage was adopted to detract the attention of the fighting men from the quantity of their blood that was being splashed about them. Whether the *Cutty Sark* adhered to the old tradition or not I have not been able to find out, so while regretting the loss of a little excusable bright colour about her decks, I have stuck to her modern grey waterways.

Making the Waterways.—They run the entire length of the deck, and require a considerable sweep at the forward end to fit the shape of the ship, but run more or less straight aft. I made each waterway in one piece, and had to think out some dodge of hollowing them out, so as to get an even concavity all the way along. Scooping them out with a gouge and sand-papering after might give the desired result in the hands of a skilled man, but I knew I should not get them even and regular enough in that way. The lathe solved the difficulty quite satisfactorily. With the circular saw, two pieces well over the length required, and $\frac{7}{16}$ in. exactly in width, were cut from an old venetian-blind slat $\frac{1}{8}$ in. thick. (In passing, I may mention again that old

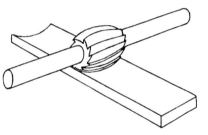

Fig. 23.—A Simple Form of Milling Cutter made from a Scrap of Silver Steel for forming the Concave Contour of the Waterways.

venetian blinds are most useful material for the model maker for all sorts of purposes, being absolutely dry, knotless, and straight-grained.) A flat block of wood was bolted on to the saddle, and two guide pieces, also of blind slat, tacked on to the top of this block far enough apart to allow the $\frac{7}{16}$-in. strips to slide between them at right angles to the bed of the lathe. It was then necessary to make a tool to do the scooping out (v. Fig. 23). A $\frac{1}{2}$-in. piece of round silver steel was cut off, faced, centred, and drilled to take a $\frac{1}{4}$-in. mandrel, fitted to the mandrel and then turned down between centres to a fat elliptical contour. Cutting teeth were then filed ; there was no need to harden it. This is

one of the numerous occasions when one spends a couple
of hours fixing things to do a five minutes' job. The flat
block of wood with its guides was adjusted to the level to
secure the desired cut, and after a trial trip with a bit of
scrap, the $\frac{7}{16}$-in. strips were pushed through : the beginning and end of the cut was a little ragged, hence the
desirability of using the over-length strips. After a gentle
rub with fine sand-paper on a suitably curved bit of wood
the result was quite satisfactory. These waterways were
painted with several coats of grey sanding filler and rubbed
down smooth, which gives the exact and somewhat mottled
appearance of cement.

Fitting the Waterways.—The waterways must now be
placed in position, but before doing so insert between
them and the $\frac{1}{8}$-in. square strip a $\frac{1}{4}$-in. strip of $\frac{1}{32}$-in. 3-ply,
or whatever other material is to be used for the bulwarks.
When this is removed later there will be space for the
bulwarks to slip in. At the after end the waterway butts
against the poop block, the front of which is, as previously
mentioned, covered by a piece of $\frac{1}{32}$-in. 3-ply ; put a piece
there temporarily. Similarly, a temporary packing is
needed at the fore end where the waterway comes against
the block which supports the after edge of the forecastle
deck. To fit against this the front edge of the waterway
must be cut slightly diagonally. Screw down the fore
end and then bend the waterway to the right curve, and
cut off the after end so that it is of exactly the right length.
It can then be sprung into position, and its natural
tendency to spring out will keep it pressed against the
$\frac{1}{32}$-in. strip and the $\frac{1}{8}$-in. packing strip lying outside of it.
If, owing to the curve of the sheer, you find it has a
tendency to rise, put in one or two more $\frac{1}{4}$-in. screws, but
consult the diagram showing the bulwark layout for the
position of these screws. They will be replaced later on
by screws made to imitate ring bolts.

The Under Deck.—The next proceeding is to cut out

and fit what may be called the under deck, on which the actual deck planking is to be laid. On the whole, I think $\frac{1}{16}$-in. 3-ply is the best material to use for this, as when the glue is put on it has less tendency to buckle than any plain sheet. This under deck must be made to fit close up against the inner edges of the waterways, and it must be given a camber, or, in other words, a slight convexity upwards, from side to side.

The Deck Beams.—The camber is obtained by screwing on to the under side of the deck a number of deck beams. Eight or ten of these beams are used. The camber given to each beam is $\frac{5}{32}$ in., that is, they are $\frac{5}{32}$ in. higher in the centre than at the ends. Cut one as a pattern and use it as a template for the others so that the beams will all have the same curvature. As they do not support the deck they may be cut a little bit short, so that they will slip into their places easily. In arranging their positions see that they clear the mast housings and the pumps. Each deck beam is screwed firmly on to the deck with four $\frac{1}{4}$-in. screws, the countersunk heads of which are on the deck. If the deck has been made a close fit to the waterways, it will become an easy fit when screwed on to the deck beams, as its centre has now been lifted up. The under deck should extend for about 3 in. under the forecastle head.

The camber, however, stiffens the deck in the fore and aft direction, so that it no longer takes the curve of the sheer readily, but if a heavy weight is placed on it amidships it will sink down all right.

Fixation of Under Deck.—Now look at the diagram of the bulwark layout and you will see two pairs of bollards on the main deck, one pair about the level of the foremast, and the other pair about the level of the after end of the after deck house. These bollards are, fortunately, most conveniently placed to cover up screws. Take the deck off and screw on to the inside of the hull a small piece of wood under the position of the bollards, and mark off on the deck the centres of these positions. Replace the deck with the weight amidships, see that it is bedded down along both edges, and screw it down with four screws. If not quite satisfactory, put in two more screws about the level of the main mast : these screws can be covered later by the chocks which hold the spare spars. On removal of the weight the deck will now retain both the camber and the sheer.

Marking the Centre Line of the Deck.—The next proceeding is to mark out the centre line of the deck, and this must be very carefully done with a pair of dividers from the edge of the waterways. In order to get this measurement right, the waterways should previously be lightly pencilled at each station line, which will be found inside the hull, otherwise the dividers may mark centre points on an oblique instead of on a true transverse line. It is also useful to mark on the deck several transverse lines, which will, of course, all be parallel. Having found the centre point in, say, half a dozen places, scribe in the centre line and pencil it.

Marking Out the Deck.—Now mark on this line the positions of the masts, the deck houses, and the hatches. Take off the deck and mark out the exact sizes of all these, and check the markings for squareness. When you are certain that the lines are square and in their proper relative positions, cut the mast holes ; these can be quite $\frac{7}{8}$ in. in diameter. When cutting out the openings for the hatches do not cut on the lines, but about $\frac{1}{8}$ in. inside, so as to leave a little shelf for the hatch coaming to rest upon. Openings may also be cut under the deck houses, leaving a shelf as before, because it is convenient to have the $\frac{3}{16}$-in. bolts, which pass through the gun-metal supports for the model, in a position where they can be got at if necessary. After these openings have been cut, replace the deck. The screw holes register its position, so that

its centre line will always be true, and it will be found to
fit the sheer line more easily now that the openings have
been cut. If it happens that a deck beam comes under
one of the openings, the beam must not be cut (*v.* Fig. 24).

Material for Deck Planking.—The planking can now
be prepared. There is a choice of two timbers, either of
which is, generally speaking, correct for the deck planking
of this class of ship. The choice lies between teak and
yellow pine. The *Cutty Sark's* deck was of teak, but
many contemporary ships had decks of yellow pine. Decks
of modern high-class steamers are, almost without excep-

FIG. 24.—The Model on its Side, with Deck Houses, Hatches, etc., removed
to show the various Openings in the Deck. A shelf is left inside the deck
planking to form a seating for the houses, etc.

tion, laid in teak. Owing to the amount of oil it contains
it is extremely durable, and exposure to the sun and air
bleaches it to a soft light grey colour, although when
new, and when wet, it is brown. Yellow pine is now scarce,
and therefore expensive. It is a beautifully straight-
grained timber and practically without a knot. It is, I
believe, still used for the decks of high-class yachts. For
a model nothing could be nicer than a yellow-pine deck,
it will take a beautiful finish, and the contrast with the
black caulking lines shows up extremely well. However,
the *Cutty Sark's* decks were laid in teak, and though I
felt very much drawn to the prettier looking yellow pine,
I happened to come into possession of a small piece of the

ship's original teak deck, and that, as the saying is, "put the lid on it." In a way I felt beholden to old Captain Moodie, who is said to have rejected so much of the builders' material, for it would be impossible to find a nicer bit of teak, and even to-day it is full of oil.

The Margin Plank.—Having chosen and secured the timber for the deck planking, cut first of all several long strips $\frac{3}{16}$ in. wide and $\frac{1}{16}$ in. thick. The outside plank of a deck is called the covering board or margin plank, and is usually 8 or 9 in. wide. Lay this margin plank first, pressing it well up against the edge of the waterways. As this edge is $\frac{1}{8}$ in. thick and the under deck is $\frac{1}{16}$ in., the top of the teak margin plank comes flush with the waterways. Glue and pin it down in position, but do not let the glue stick to the waterways. This can be prevented by running a bit of very thin copper shim between the two before the glue sets.

Laying Surrounds for the Deck Openings.—Mitred surrounds for the deck houses and hatches are now laid, also of the $\frac{3}{16}$ in. strip. These surrounds must be laid exactly to the scribed lines, and the easiest way to do it is to have the hatches and deck houses, or at any rate the carcass of them, already made, and to lay the surrounds up to them. When laying these surrounds take every precaution, by checking off their edges, both to the centre line and to the margin plank, to make certain that they are true. As the deck houses are both of the same width, the long sides of their surrounds should be in the same straight line. Cut the mitres as clean as you can, and for this purpose it is a good thing to make a little mitre box in which you can saw the strips accurately. Do not glue the surrounds at present, but pin them down only. There are small mitred squares at the foot of the masts. They are made by glueing the four small mitred strips on to a piece of paper with black paper inlay (shortly to be described), and then boring a $\frac{3}{4}$-in. hole in their centres.

The pumps also stand on a mitred base. Although the masts are $\frac{5}{8}$ in. in diameter the holes in the deck are made larger in order to take the mast coats. It is as well to make these at this juncture, so that the masts with their coats and mitred surrounds can be put in their proper positions : the latter can be glued and pinned down permanently.

Cutting the Deck Planking.—Now make the deck planking proper. Each plank will be 5 in. long, $\frac{1}{16}$ in. thick, and a shade under $\frac{1}{8}$ in. wide. To cut these planks proceed as follows :—

Say the piece of timber is about 4 in. by 3 in. Pieces exactly 5 in. long are cut off and squared at the ends. Each piece is then cut by the circular saw into slabs just under $\frac{1}{8}$ in. thick. After setting the fence of the saw to $\frac{1}{16}$ in., each slab is cut into strips, thus obtaining planks $\frac{1}{8}$ in. bare wide, $\frac{1}{16}$ in. thick, and 5 in. long.

Laying the Planks.—The planks must be laid from the middle outwards, and from aft forwards. In order to obtain a shipshape deck it is essential that the planks should run in a straight line fore and aft, any waviness in the lines will be accentuated as the planking nears the waterways, so it is worth while to take one's time in making sure that the first few lines of planking are really straight. It is quite easy to do this by putting a straightedge against the longitudinal members of the surrounds of the deck houses and filling in the gaps with temporary battens tacked to the deck. This gives a solid straight edge to lay the first planks against.

Caulking the Deck.—Then comes the question of caulking the planks. In a real ship the edges of the planks are cut with a very slight bevel, so that when two planks are placed side by side the lower edges touch but the upper edges are separated by a V-shaped gap about $\frac{1}{4}$ in. wide. Into the space left the caulking material, tow, or what not, is hammered with a caulking tool, and hot liquid pitch is poured on top to fill the seam and make it watertight.   When dry and hard the pitch is scraped off, leaving a straight black line $\frac{1}{4}$ in. wide between the planks.   The butts of the planks and all mitred joints are treated similarly.

There are several ways of imitating this caulking in model work.   Perhaps the simplest and least troublesome of the effective methods I tried is the one I finally adopted, and that is to glue a strip of black paper between each plank and each butt.   There is a kind of black stiff paper, sold in reels about 1 in. wide, which is used for *passe-partout* framing.   It can generally be obtained at any photographic stores, and when cut in strips about $\frac{1}{8}$ in. wide answers the purpose admirably.

First Stage in Laying the Deck.—Lay the first plank against the batten, with its after end against the break of the poop, by glueing it to the under deck, and carry on with 5-in. planks up to the forecastle, remembering to lay a $\frac{1}{8}$-in. strip of black paper between each butt.   If any of the planks do not lie solid on the deck, drill a hole and put a pin through to hold it down.   I used thin brass $\frac{1}{2}$-in. pins.   Be careful where you drill the hole, and drill it with a small twist drill so as not to split the plank. When the brass pin is taken out later, the hole will be occupied by a dowel, and as these dowel holes run in lines across the deck their positions must be thought out.   I spaced mine 1 in. apart, so that each plank is dowelled at 2, 3, and 4 in., and each has a dowel $\frac{1}{8}$ in. from each end.

Start, then, on the second row of planks, and here it is wise to watch your step.   The first plank of the second row must be 2 in. long, the sequence to get the correct layout of the planking being 5, 2, 4, 1, 3 (*v.* Fig. 22), that is, taking the planks butting against the break of the poop from within outwards, the first is 5 in. long, the second 2 in., the third 4 in., and so on.   Once you start correctly from the after end the pattern works out automatically, and you go on laying 5-in. planks.

There is just a small precaution to be observed here, which I learnt after I had finished laying my deck—I did not get all my butts dead straight across the deck for this reason. All my 5-in. planks were of exactly the same length, being cut off blocks carefully measured and faced up, but I was not careful enough about the 2, 4, 1, and 3 in. ones. Only a few are needed, but if I ever lay another deck I shall be very careful to see that they are cut to their exact length. Obviously, if they are only a little bit short, they will throw out the symmetry of the pattern, so cut the 2, 4, 1, and 3-in. planks dead right.

The First Caulking Strip.—Now glue a long strip of black paper against the outer edge of the first row of planks. The black paper is very curly, but if you run it over the edge of your thumb-nail it behaves quite reasonably; its upper edge will, of course, project above the level of the planking, but that does not matter, as it will be scraped off later. Against this lay your 2-in. plank aft, following on by fives till you get to the forecastle. Then another long strip of black paper and the 4-in. plank aft, and so on, not forgetting the butts. I want to make it quite plain without being wearisome. Continue with the parallel lines of planking until the curvature of the margin plank stops any more parallel rows being laid, and then treat the other side of the deck in the same way. It will take a bit of time, and by the time you have finished the other side the glue on the first side will be set, and you will not be able to resist the temptation of scraping off the upstanding edges of black paper to see how the deck looks. You will be very pleased with the result.

Laying the Central Planks.—After laying both sides up to the margin plank take out the temporary battens, which have acted as straightedges, and proceed to fill up the spaces left in the centre of the deck, cutting the planking to the length necessary to fill up the various gaps. This is so simple that it requires no explanation. The only hint I should like to give about this point is, not to use more liquid glue than you can help, because there will be a tendency for the under deck to buckle towards the centre : prevent this by laying fairly heavy weights on the deck. All the mitre joints, and joints between the planking and surrounds of hatches, etc., should now be filled with black paper before glueing down.

The Filling-in Boards.—Now we come to a more tricky part of it. Unless the planks have been cut dead accurate as regards width, and have been laid exactly, the gap between the outermost plank and the margin plank will not be the same on each side. In my deck the gap was $\frac{3}{64}$ in. more on the starboard side than on the port side. This gap is occupied by what the shipwright calls " filling-in boards," and he will generally aim at using two narrow filling-in boards rather than one wide one, so exercise your discretion similarly. If the gap is wider than $\frac{1}{8}$ in., cut a board to fill it, then slit it in two with the fine circular saw and fill in the gap, the black paper taking up the space made by the saw cut between the two bits.

Joggling the Planks.—The next bit of work is really fascinating, and consists in joggling the ends of the planks into the margin plank at the curvature running towards the bows. (In some ships a separate joggling plank is laid inside the margin plank, which is left untouched.) If you have a chance, go on board a ship and have a look at the planking on, say, the forecastle head. Where the straight fore and aft planking meets the rounded margin plank it is joggled in.

Rules for Joggling.—There are two shipwright's rules about this joggling.

1. The square end of the joggled plank must be half the width of the plank.

2. A plank must be joggled when the " snipe " is more than twice the width of the plank.

This, I may tell you, is straight from the horse's mouth.

The " snipe " is the technical term used for the length of the diagonal cut across the width of a plank made to fit it into an angle. It is necessary to know this rule in order to know when a plank should be joggled and when not. You will notice on a forecastle head or round the stern of a ship that some of the planks are joggled and some are not (*v.* Fig. 25). In such an ancient trade as shipbuilding none of these things is done by accident, there is always some rule to guide you, and this second rule about the " snipe " is the one in this instance. In our model, therefore, where the diagonal cut across a plank would come to more than

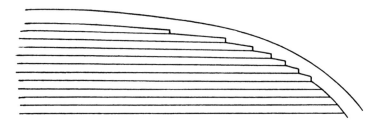

Fig. 25.—Deck Planking of the Poop, illustrating the Rules concerning the Joggling of Deck Planks into a Curved Margin Plank.

$\frac{1}{4}$ in., that plank must be joggled. A glance at the diagram will make the principle of the thing quite clear. To carry it out proceed as follows :—

Place the plank to be joggled with its forward end projecting over the curve of the margin plank. Mark the exact spots where the inner and outer edges of the plank first touch the margin plank. (In order to mark these fine points, rub a little chalk on the plank first.) Cut the plank off square at the mark on the inner edge. Draw a diagonal line from the mark on the outer edge to the central point of the squared end, and cut away the wood in front of this line. Now put the shaped plank in position, mark the position of its end on the margin plank, and cut a notch for it in the margin plank, so that the shaped plank fits in. It is better to cut and fit all the joggled planks before glueing any of them down permanently. The joggles on the two sides should be symmetrical, of course.

Scraping the Deck.—When this has been finished the deck is ready for scraping. All the upstanding edges of the black paper are cut away, and if any edges of the planks project they can be rubbed down with sand-paper. Be careful not to rub hollows in the deck. A touch with a sharp scraper here and there improves the look of it.

Dowelling the Deck.—The next proceeding is the dowelling: rather a tedious job. A series of holes $\frac{1}{32}$ in. must be bored through the planks and underlying deck. Each row of holes run straight across the deck, and each row is an inch apart in the fore and aft direction. At the butts the holes are $\frac{1}{8}$ in. from the ends of the planks. I know of no way of relieving the tedium of this job, but it is one of those repetition jobs which should not be gone on with too long. One gets tired or careless, and very apt to make mistakes which may spoil the whole thing, so do a bit at a time, and knock off when you are getting tired of it. I found a small twist drill held in a jeweller's pin tongs the best tool, and marked each hole first with a sharp pricker.

Making the Dowel Rod.—Then comes the question of the dowels. For a real deck the dowels are cut from a thick plank by a revolving cutter with a serrated edge. It must be remembered that they are there for covering the heads of the bolts, and strength is not required. If the dowels were cut off from a rounded rod they would show end grain and be different in colour, so that the deck would be covered with spots. It is not, however, necessary to carry out this refinement for model work. I do not think you can buy anywhere a close-grained rod $\frac{1}{32}$ in. in diameter. I thought of using surgical fishing gut at one time, but I finally used boxwood for the dowels.

At any cabinetmakers you can buy, or he will tell

you where to buy, a trade article known as boxwood
stringing. If you have a fine circular saw it is quite easy
to run it out yourself. It is square boxwood strip about
$\frac{3}{64}$ in. square, and in 3-ft. lengths, a shilling a dozen. This
strip can be drawn like wire through a draw-plate. The
ordinary wire draw-plate does not work with it. Get a
scrap of fairly stout tin-plate, drill a series of holes diminish-
ing in size from, say, $\frac{1}{16}$ to $\frac{1}{32}$ in. by half a dozen gradations,
smooth down the rough edges, and you have a perfectly
satisfactory draw-plate. I cut the 3-ft. strips in half
before drawing them. In this way you can get perfectly
rounded and uniform dowel rods of any size you like.

You must then proceed to fill up all the holes with
dowels—another tedious job. Twist the end of the rod
into the hole, cut it off about $\frac{1}{8}$ in. above the deck, and
knock it in. I do not think it is necessary to glue the
dowels, as the knocking spreads their heads a little, but
when all is finished and you subsequently lift the deck
off, brush over with glue the projecting ends of the dowels
on the under side of the deck. Any projecting ends on
the upper surface are cut off, and the whole deck rubbed
down with fine sand-paper and scraped.

I should mention that small gaps must be left in the
planking over the heads of the screws which hold the
deck down.

Teak having a somewhat open grain in parts, it is
advisable to fill it. Beeswax and turpentine will do this,
but as a deck is not, anyhow primarily, a ballroom floor,
it should not be polished too highly.

The beeswax is a good filler for the open grain. Get
it to a soft paste with turpentine and rub into the deck
with a palette knife, working it in thoroughly. Scrape off
the excess and give it a rub with a turpentine rag. Teak
feeds well on the beeswax, and more than one coating will
be needed. Do not aim at a high polish; a clear matt
effect is what is needed. It will be found that after the

Fig. 26.—Close-up View of Deck of Model to show Planking. The method of joggling the planking into the margin plank can just be seen in some places. Note the anchor release gear on the fore side of the catheads. Outside the bulwarks, opposite the fore mast, the fore ends of the swinging booms can be seen. The windlass itself is under the forecastle deck.

planking is complete and the glue perfectly dry that the deck retains its camber, and the fore and aft sheer very well. For this reason the planking must be done with the deck in position.

Besides the main deck, the poop and forecastle head are decked in the same way. Lay out the mitred surrounds for the coach-house top first, and fill in round this. The margin plank is formed by the main rail continued aft as far as it can be bent. Round the stern itself, shaped pieces must be cut out. I used three pieces to get round. About five planks require joggling. The planks in front of the coach-house top run athwartships to the companion-way. The photograph (Fig. 26) was taken from the model to show some of the details of the deck planking.

CHAPTER VII.

SOLDERING.

In making up the fittings and ironwork of the ship it is necessary to become fairly expert in joining together bits of metal. If there is any strain at all on any of the parts, hard soldering must be employed. For instance, in making a mast band with eyes, the area of contact between the two pieces is so small that a slight pull may detach the eye if soft soldered, and nothing could be more annoying were such an accident to occur when the rigging has arrived at an advanced stage. Such a contretemps will never happen if the parts are hard soldered; there is no more difficulty about the latter than there is in soft soldering.

Hard or Silver Soldering.—Silver solder is a mixture of tin and silver; the higher the proportion of tin the easier it runs. A large variety of grades of silver solder can be obtained from Grays, 18 Clerkenwell Road; the price varies with the market price of silver, but is roughly about 3s. 6d. an ounce. An ounce goes a very long way: I do not think I have used as much as half an ounce in the whole of this model.

It is generally sold in a thin sheet. For use, cut it with a pair of scissors into strips about $\frac{1}{16}$ in. wide, and cut the strip into small lengths about $\frac{1}{16}$ in. I have also used silver wire a good deal. It does not run quite so readily as a silver solder, but it is convenient to use at times.

The flux used must be borax in some form. I have

had a tin of boron compound, from Gray's, 1s. a tin, for a long time, and I seem to make very little impression upon its contents. Have a watch glass, or one of those hollowed glass blocks dentists make their little mixtures in, and grind up a little boron compound, which is blue, into a thin paste with water. A fine paint brush is useful for applying it to small parts.

In silver soldering, the parts must be brought to a bright red heat, and it is on this account that some experience and skill is necessary when dealing with small articles, owing to the tendency of the metal to melt. A lot of the brass wire and small brass sections obtainable from model supply houses melt very easily, therefore make a point of using copper or bronze whenever you can. One can, of course, hard solder small bits of brass, but a whiff too much down the blow-pipe may ruin a bit of work all too quickly.

A small gas blow-pipe is the most convenient heating apparatus, and for all small work the mouth is the best and most controllable bellows. The blow-pipe should have a tap to regulate the flame.

The two things I have come to regard as most important to ensure success are—firstly, that the points to be joined must be in contact, and, secondly, must be clean. There are, for instance, umpteen eyes about the ship. I usually bend them up from copper wire, leaving a shank. The cut end of the wire forming the loop of the eye should be soldered on to the shank, but you will find that if there is the slightest air space between, the solder will refuse to bridge across it. If the points are in metallic contact with each other there is no difficulty, therefore see that the parts are touching; if you are in doubt, hold them up between your eye and the light.

The only real difficulty about soldering is found in holding the pieces in position. With the odd shapes and sizes one has to deal with this is a very real difficulty, and it is a matter for the individual exercise of intelligence. Many articles can easily be wired together—use thin iron wire. Gray's sell a special brand of carbon iron wire for this purpose, which does not melt. There is a most useful little tool, costing 2s. 6d., used, according to the catalogues, for holding spectacle frames together while being mended. It is a bar with a wooden handle ; on the bar are mounted two clips with universal joints, by which you can hold almost anything in any relative position. I use also a block of charcoal and a bit of asbestos sheet (which was a stove mat discarded from the kitchen); obtainable at any ironmongers for a few pence. A few bits of broken gas-fire radiants also come in handy at times.

One very great advantage of hard soldering is that once a part is stuck on it very seldom comes off again if you have to reheat the piece in order to attach another bit. Take, for instance, the mast band found at the foot of the mast. This band is hinged, and to make it the hinged pieces must be attached first. Then there are five separate eyes on each side, four of which are of such a shape that it is almost impossible to avoid attaching them one by one ; if one tried to do this job with soft solder, three would drop off while one was attaching one.

The actual process is quite easy : if you can get a friend to show you, it will be understood more readily than by reading any description. Say, for instance, you want to solder the ball head on to a davit. You have the ball drilled and the davit end fitted into the hole. Paint round the line of union with the boron paste ; a minute amount does all that is necessary so long as it covers all the joint. Bend up a tiny bit of silver wire : this is more likely to stay in position than a bit of ordinary silver solder. Now approach the flame—quite small—of the blow-pipe to the part. The first thing that happens is that the boron bubbles up and dislodges the silver, unless you are careful.

By gently warming the part with the blow-pipe first, you get the boron to solidify, and in doing so you can generally manage so that it fixes the silver in its grip. Once that has happened you can blow away till the parts get red hot ; both the parts to be joined must get red hot. Now watch out and keep your eye on the silver. Quite suddenly it will melt and run wherever the boron lets it, and you will see it shining very brightly in its molten condition. As soon as you see this brightness, stop blowing ; you cannot improve matters by applying more heat, and it is just the extra whiff at this stage which will melt a bit of brass. Let it cool down until the redness disappears ; pick it up with forceps and drop it into weak sulphuric acid. Leave it there for five minutes, rinse with water, dry in boxwood dust, and rub over with a wire scratch-brush. The critical moment of the process is when you see the silver melt and run actively over the part.

I might mention here that if you want to clean a piece of metal before soldering, and it is not convenient to do it in some other way, an easy way to clean it is to heat it, drop it into weak sulphuric acid pickle, and then give it a rub with the scratch-brush. Copper can be cleaned by heating to redness and dropping it into alcohol.

Soft Soldering.—The process of soft soldering is so well known that it is hardly necessary to give any description of it here. Suffice it to say that the two essentials previously mentioned for hard soldering are necessary for soft solder-ing, and more particularly the cleanliness of the metal. There is on the market a product which I have found extremely useful and which apparently is not at all widely known. It is a paste composed of soft solder, in various strengths, and a flux combined. For small work it is very handy, since it sticks on the part where it is put, and also helps to hold the parts together. A whiff with a blow-pipe suffices to make it run, but apply the flame not to the paste but to the metal round. The paste is called Britinol, and can be obtained at the price of a shilling a tube from most tool dealers. If soft solder spreads itself where it is not wanted, I know of no way to clean it off except with a file ; there is no chemical which will remove the stain. If you use a scratch-brush on soft-soldered work do not use it for other work, as it will give it a dull, leaden look.

CHAPTER VIII.

THE BULWARKS.

THE construction of the bulwarks is an interesting part of the work and one which may be undertaken in several different ways. I will first describe their structure in the actual ship, and the reader will then understand the problem which faces him.

Structure of Bulwarks.—The main-deck bulwarks are 5 ft. 3 in. overall in height amidships. At the break of the poop, and of the forecastle, they are 5 ft. 6 in. high. Amidships they slope inwards slightly to correspond with the tumble-home of the midship section. Towards the forecastle they slope outwards, and at the break of the poop they are practically vertical. The bulwarks consist of a lower and of an upper section divided by the main rail. The lower section is 4 ft. high and the upper 15 in. : the former is built of $\frac{5}{16}$-in. iron plates and the latter of timber. The main rail is made of teak.

Running along the edge of the main deck there is a stringer of angle-iron, which is riveted to the deck beams beneath it. Iron plates about 4 ft. high and 15 ft. long are riveted to the outer face of the vertical member of this angle. At the middle and at the joints of the plates, butt straps 9 in. wide are riveted inside the bulwarks, so that their outer surface is flush. Each butt strap is supported by a stout stanchion or bulwark stay. These stanchions run diagonally upwards and outwards from the inner edge of the waterways to the top of the strap, where they are bent over and flattened into a palm to give support to the main rail. About half-way along their length a horizontal stiffening rod, technically known as the " spur," is welded on, which runs outwards, and ends in a short, flat horizontal palm, which is riveted on to the butt strap.

The Main Rail.—The main rail is a solid plank of teak 12 in. wide and 4 in. thick, which is bolted on to the bent-over heads of the bulwark stanchions. There is also an angle-iron at the top of the bulwark plates joining them to the main rail. On the outer edge of the main rail there is fixed vertically a plank 12 in. high and panelled on the inside ; on the top of this there is a rounded wooden rail about 4 in. deep. This is called the topgallant, or simply, the top rail.

Such, roughly, is a general idea of the actual structure of the main-deck bulwarks.

All the lower shrouds and backstays are fixed to the iron plates which form the bulwark. The lower dead-eyes are situated just above the main rail. Their strops are bolted to steel shanks which pass through the main rail, and end in square plates or palms about 9 in. across. These palms are riveted inside the iron bulwark plates. The rigging has no other attachment to the hull. The arrangement does not, at first sight, appear to err on the side of strength, but it has stood the test of time. The usual arrangement in later steel sailing ships was slightly different. The sheer strake, which is the top strake of the hull plating, and thicker than the rest of the plating, extended about a foot above the main-deck level. The palms of the rigging screw shanks were riveted to the inside of the sheer strake, and the thinner bulwark plating was riveted outside.

Openings of Bulwarks.—The bulwarks are penetrated by certain openings. There is an oval hawse hole or mooring port, 18 in. long by 10 in. high, close to the break of the poop, and another about 15 ft. abaft the break of the forecastle. There are six large clearing ports, 2 ft. 2 in. square on each side, and also the sheave holes for the fore and main sheets. The sheave block for the fore sheet is situated opposite the after end of the fore-deck house, and the one for the main sheet is 13 ft. 9 in. from the break of the poop. Under the fore and the main rigging the main rail is 6 in. wider, and has numerous holes for belaying pins.

Methods of Construction.—Different methods of constructing the bulwarks will immediately occur to the model builder. The pros and cons for each method must be weighed up. I hesitated for some time between a wood and a metal bulwark. My main idea was to get the whole main-deck bulwark in one piece, so that it would not show any joints on the outside. The metal bulwark has this great advantage, that the dead-eye palms can be riveted directly to it, as in the actual ship. There are, however, difficulties about fixing the rails and mouldings to a metal bulwark. I made some trial attempts at flanging over copper strips for the lower part of the bulwarks, but not being an expert sheet-metal worker I came to the conclusion that I could get a better result in other ways. I generally found that my flanged strips were concave outwards, whereas one wants to get them concave upwards and slightly convex outwards. I expect, however, that with a little perseverance this difficulty could have been overcome.

I will therefore describe the bulwarks as constructed in my model; in their appearance they depart from the original in only one particular, and that is in the way the dead-eye palms are fixed. Anyone not intimately acquainted with the ship would, I think, hardly notice this variation.

Fixation of Waterways.—It will be remembered that the waterways, each $\frac{7}{16}$ in. wide and $\frac{1}{8}$ in. deep, run along the outside of the main deck, and in fixing these waterways allowance was made on the outside of them for an $\frac{1}{8}$-in. square packing strip, and $\frac{1}{32}$ in. for the bulwarks between the two. The waterways must be really solidly fixed, and there is nothing like a few screws for doing this : one cannot rely upon glue. The little problem then arose as to how to hide the screws. This difficulty was got over by making the screws appear to be something else ; as described in the section on ring bolts, they were made to resemble these necessary fittings, and at the same time held the waterways absolutely solid (v. Fig. 27).

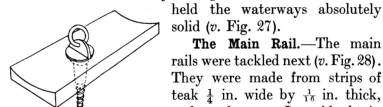

FIG. 27.—A very Useful Form of Ring-bolt, made from a $\frac{1}{4}$-in. Wood Screw and used for Fixing the Waterways.

The Main Rail.—The main rails were tackled next (v. Fig. 28). They were made from strips of teak $\frac{1}{4}$ in. wide by $\frac{1}{16}$ in. thick, and as long as I could obtain them, from the piece of the ship's teak which was given to me. The fore end of each strip was housed in a slot cut on the after side of the knightheads (v. Fig. 6). The strips were then bent round the forecastle head and pinned to the blocks on which the forecastle deck rests. Careful measurements were made from the centre line to the strip to make sure that their curvature was symmetrical. They were then carried back to about the level of the after-deck house. Strips of wood were laid across the deck at intervals, and the main rail strips were pinned to these at appropriate distances apart. It took some little time for these strips of teak to accommodate themselves to the curve, but I found that by this method one obtained a long, fair, sweeping curve which one could not obtain easily by using shorter strips. Where the strips ended about the level of the after-deck house they were joined by other strips, which were continued on to the poop, where they formed the margin plank of the poop deck. The small bollards on the main rail, just abaft the main rigging, came in very handy for covering up the joint between the two pieces. In making the rail in this fashion, it will be found that there is a great tendency for the rail to slope inwards after it leaves the forecastle deck. This tendency is very easily corrected by the stanchions, as will be seen later.

The Bulwark Stays or Stanchions.—There are twenty-six of these stanchions along each side of the deck, spaced approximately 5 ft. apart, or $1\frac{1}{4}$ in. Half of these are

FIG. 28.—Side View of Model in Early Stage. Note the main rail running from forecastle head to poop; it is supported temporarily by metal strips bent up. The deck houses are unpainted, and the deck has not been laid.

just the plain stanchions with the horizontal stiffening rod or spur, as already described. In four of them there is no horizontal bar, but the stanchion is bent abruptly backwards. These stanchions are found on the fore side of the after mooring port, and on the after side of the fore mooring port, and are fashioned in this way in order to give a clear run to the hawsers from the port to the bollards on deck. The remaining stanchions have stout iron rings welded on below the horizontal bar, and some of them have a loose ring threaded through the welded ring. One pair has a cleat instead of a ring (v. Fig. 29).

Making the Stanchions.—The stanchions are made up of brass wire about $\frac{3}{64}$ in. in diameter. Brass wire is preferable to copper wire, because after heating it retains its rigidity a little bit better. Prepare two pieces of wire to solder together. The longer piece should be about $1\frac{1}{2}$ in. long, and the short one about $\frac{1}{2}$ in. File a groove diagonally in the end of the $\frac{1}{2}$-in. piece so that it will lie snug against the long piece at an angle as indicated. Place the two pieces on a bit of asbestos sheet, and keep them approximately in their correct position by a few pieces of thin copper wire, bent like staples, and holding them to the

FIG. 29.—The Five Types of Bulwark Stanchions. Reading from left to right, they are plain, single ring, double ring, cleat, and bent.

asbestos sheet. Then apply boron paste, silver solder, and the blow-pipe.

It cannot be expected that all the pieces will be soldered together at exactly the same angle, and it is therefore necessary to standardise the angle. The whole beauty of the work about these stanchions is that they shall be absolutely regular and even : it is astonishing how easily the eye will catch the slightest irregularity, and one stanchion out of shape or line may spoil the whole effect.

Standardising the Stanchion Angle.—The angles can be corrected with the greatest ease. Take a piece of wood about $\frac{1}{4}$ in. thick : boxwood is best for this little jig (v. Fig. 30). Drill a hole through it diagonally at the angle of the stanchion, and at the top of this hole scoop out a little hollow. All that need be done is to pass the short

bar of the stanchion through the hole and press down
the longer bar on the surface of the boxwood. After the
heating, the brass will be quite amenable. While held in
this jig they may be scratch-brushed. Half the stanchions
are thus very easily and quickly made. Those which have
rings and cleats must be heated up again, and the accessories soldered on in their correct position. In doing this
there is very little danger of the wires coming apart. It
did not occur once while I was
making mine.

The Butt Straps.—The next
things to make are the butt straps.
These are made with $\frac{1}{4}$ in., bent
over at the top, to go underneath
and support the main rail. In

Fig. 30.—Simple Jig for Standardising the Angle of the
Bulwark Stanchions.

the real ship the top of the stanchion is bent over and flattened out to form a palm, but for model purposes a better
support, and one more easily made, is obtained by flanging
over the top of the butt straps. Now these have got to
be all of the same size, except a few to be mentioned
shortly. Therefore the quickest and surest way of making
them is to make one or two little jigs, in which to cut
them off to the right length, and to bend them at the
correct spot. Such jigs are so simple that they really need
no description. The length of the vertical part of the
strap is 1 in. plus $\frac{1}{8}$ in. for the thickness of the waterway,
minus $\frac{1}{16}$ in. for the thickness of the main rail and $\frac{1}{32}$ in.
for the thickness of the metal in turning over the angle.
Each strap should therefore be bent at exactly $1\frac{1}{32}$ in.
from the end. They are bent up of brass strips $\frac{3}{16}$ in. by
$\frac{1}{32}$ in.

Holes in Straps.—Three holes are drilled in each strap;
one hole is drilled in the angle to take the top end, and
one about the centre to take the spur, of the stanchion. A
third smaller hole, countersunk on the outer side, is drilled
$\frac{1}{16}$ in. from the bottom. This is a small hole to take a

copper rivet for fixing the strap to the waterways. These holes are drilled through a jig. This jig is simply a strip of the same brass with a hole drilled centrally. Put one of the straps with the angle upwards between two strips of wood $\frac{1}{8}$ in. high nailed to a small board. Put the jig on the top of the strap, push it up to the angle, and drill the hole. If the end of the jig is tight up against the angle, the position of the hole in the straps will always be the same, and being held by the strips of wood, it cannot be more to one side than the other.

Cutting the Stanchions to Length.—The stanchions are now cut so that the upper leg and the horizontal bar fill the holes in the straps without projecting beyond their surface. Yet another jig is required to accomplish this. This jig is made of one of the straps already drilled. File away one side of the angle so that the top leg of the stanchions can slip in (*v.* Fig. 31). As long as the legs are uncut, they cannot be put into both holes of the straps. Put the horizontal leg into its hole in the jig, and then slip in the top leg through the slot filed in the angle. Snip off the redundant portion and file the ends flat. Under this treatment any stanchion ought to fit any strap. The stanchions are now soldered to the straps. The lower leg of the stanchion is cut off level with the lower end of the strap.

Special Stanchions.—The straps and stanchions at the poop end increase very slightly in length, so that the last one is $\frac{1}{16}$ in. higher than the centre ones. It will be found, if the last four stanchions be progressively increased in length, that the desired effect will be obtained. The same procedure is necessary at the forecastle end, but here, in addition, there is the outward flare of the bulwarks to be allowed for. This is managed by bending the flange of the strap considerably beyond a right angle for the first strap, and each of the next three straps a little bit less, so that the fifth is a normal one. It is prudent to slip these special stanchions and their straps into their positions temporarily before soldering them together, to make sure that their angles are true.

The stanchions are now cleaned, silver-plated, and oxidised. While this process is being carried out take a pair of dividers and mark out points $1\frac{1}{4}$ in. apart $\frac{1}{16}$ in. from the inner edge of the waterways.

 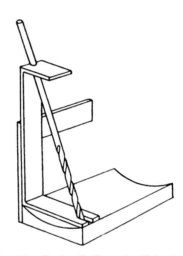

FIG. 31.—Jig for Cutting the Bulwark Stanchions to the Right Length.

FIG. 32.—Jig for Drilling the Holes in the Waterways for the Legs of the Bulwark Stanchions.

Jig for Drilling the Stanchion Sockets.—One more jig, and this is really the last one and about the most important of the lot, must be made.

This jig consists of a strip bent at two right angles, and of such a length that it will fit between the waterways and the main rail. The upper angle is drilled in the same manner as the straps. The foot piece is drilled at the same angle, $\frac{3}{8}$ in. from the back of the jig. A drill passed through the two holes will take the line of the long bar of one of the stanchions. To the back of this jig solder on a smaller strip projecting $\frac{1}{8}$ in. below its lower angle,

and another bit on one side which enables one to hold it
more easily when in use (v. Fig. 32). The object of this
jig is to give a true hole for the lower leg of the stanchions
in the waterways. The jig ensures that the holes are all
at the same distance from the edge of the waterways and
also at the correct angle. To use it, press the jig against
the outer edge of the waterways, and get the hole in the
foot exactly over one of the points marked out, and then,
holding the drill in a pin vice, make the hole.

The stanchions are then slipped in sideways, the lower
leg being placed in its hole first. If one attempts to drill
these holes without this little jig they are almost certain
to be out of line ; at any rate I would, so to speak, take
off my hat to anyone who could drill them true without
a jig.

Before fixing the stanchions in position, the dead-eyes
and their plates for the fore and main rigging must be
made.

Dead-eyes.—This is a convenient place to describe
the making of the dead-eyes, of which a large number are
required.

A dead-eye is a circular block of hard wood with three
holes through it. There is a groove in its circumference in
which, in the case of the lower dead-eyes, the strop, and
in the case of the upper dead-eyes, the bight of the shroud,
lies. The lower dead-eyes have a metal strop, the ends
of which are bolted to the upper extremity of the shank
which holds them to the body of the ship. A certain
amount of evolution has taken place in ships with regard
to these dead-eyes. The dead-eye itself is apparently a
very ancient device and was used in Roman days.

The Channels.—It is mainly in the methods of anchor-
ing the dead-eye to the ship that evolution has taken
place. At one time a chain was used for this purpose, and
to give a wider spread to the rigging, timbers were bolted
to the outside of the ship which were called the chain

wales, subsequently shortened to " channels." The expressions, the " fore chains," " main chains," etc., were used to designate those parts of the ship where the rigging of the fore and main masts was fixed to the hull. Chains were replaced later by two or three long oval links, and an expert is helped to date a model by the design of the channels.

The outside channels were disappearing by the time that the *Cutty Sark* was built. The dead-eyes were kept inside the bulwarks. In many ships of this period they were attached to metal straps which were bolted to the outside of the hull.

The *Thermopylæ*, for instance, had outside straps. From the model-making point of view it makes an easier job if the dead-eyes can be fixed to outside straps. Fixing them entirely inside the bulwarks is a rather more complicated affair, since they must be firm enough to withstand the pull of the rigging.

Material.—Dead-eyes were painted black, and a convenient material of which to make them is vulcanite, as it does not tend to split. They were made of lignum vitæ, I believe, in real practice. Two sizes of lower dead-eyes are required, $\frac{1}{4}$ and $\frac{3}{16}$ in. in diameter. This is slightly over scale size, but as there are so many to make, and they are difficult to make satisfactorily in sizes below $\frac{3}{16}$ in., this slight variation from the correct scale may be excused. The $\frac{1}{4}$-in. size does not look at all out of proportion.

I made the strops for both sizes out of $\frac{1}{16}$-in. half-round brass wire.

Turning the Blanks.—The first thing to do is to turn the groove in the vulcanite rod. A fine tool is needed; one that can turn out the groove and can also be used for parting off is convenient. I also kept handy a small graving tool, $\frac{1}{16}$ in. wide, to make sure that the groove was the right size for the strop.

Each dead-eye was parted off just over $\frac{1}{8}$ in. thick. After turning about a couple of dozen or so of grooved blanks, the holes were drilled. It would be a perfectly hopeless job to try to drill these holes without a jig. A little time must therefore be spent in making a jig.

Jig for Drilling Dead-eye.—Chuck a piece of $\frac{3}{4}$-in. round or hexagon brass rod, face, centre, drill $\frac{15}{64}$-in. hole $\frac{1}{8}$ in. deep, and square up the bottom of this hole with a $\frac{1}{4}$-in. end mill. The dead-eye blanks ought to fit this hole fairly tightly. If the centre has not been cleaned off the bottom of the hole, drill a central hole with a small drill— about 60—$\frac{1}{16}$ in. deep. Now part off the disc $\frac{3}{16}$ in. thick

and face the reverse side. There will be a central hole on this face.

With a pair of fine dividers mark out a circle $\frac{5}{32}$ in. in diameter ; on this circle mark out the points where the holes in the dead-eyes are to be, and drill the holes.

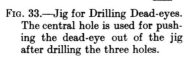

FIG. 33.—Jig for Drilling Dead-eyes. The central hole is used for pushing the dead-eye out of the jig after drilling the three holes.

Be careful to see that these holes are kept straight (*v.* Fig. 33).

Drilling the dead-eyes is now simple and quick. Push a blank into the $\frac{1}{4}$-in. hole, turn the jig over, and drill the three holes. I used a No. 58 drill ; it is a mistake to drill the holes too small.

Scoring the Holes.—The central hole is used to push out the blank after drilling. Each hole must have a small score cut to house the lanyard. At first I used a very fine carving gouge for this, but I soon gave this up in favour of a little tool bought at Woolworth's. It is a little countersink sold for countersinking vulcanite panels for wireless sets. It has a sharp point, and is perfectly useless for anything harder than vulcanite, but it makes a perfect score if the point is put in one of the dead-eye holes and twisted round, holding the tool on the slant.

The $\frac{3}{16}$-in. size of dead-eye is made in the same way and drilled through a jig, the holes being spaced on a $\frac{1}{8}$-in. circle.

Making the Strops.—The strops for the lower dead-eyes are made from $\frac{1}{16}$-in. half-round brass wire. It is advisable to heat this to redness to soften it. The groove round the $\frac{1}{4}$-in. dead-eye should be about $\frac{7}{32}$ in. in diameter. Turn a short length of brass rod to this size to act as a former on which the strops can be bent. Insert $\frac{1}{8}$ in. of the end of the half-round wire between the jaws of a vice, and give it a squeeze to flatten it ; then bend it over nearly to a right angle. Hold the $\frac{7}{32}$-in. rod on the top of it, and pull the wire over and round it to form a ring. Release the wire from the vice and cut off the long end a little beyond the short end. Then put both ends in the vice, the $\frac{7}{32}$-in. rod being still in position, and squeeze the two ends together close up against the rod ; squeeze hard enough to flatten both ends. Drill a small hole through the flattened ends and round the irregular edges with a file. It will be found that the strop will open out quite easily to admit the dead-eye.

Number of Dead-eyes.—Quite a large number are required. For the fore rigging nine $\frac{1}{4}$-in. and three $\frac{3}{16}$-in. are wanted on each side ; the main rigging has nine $\frac{1}{4}$-in. and four $\frac{3}{16}$-in., the extra one being for the skysail-mast backstay; the mizzen has seven $\frac{1}{4}$-in. and three $\frac{3}{16}$-in. ; there is no capstay, and only two topmast back-stays on the mizzen. The total required is fifty-two $\frac{1}{4}$-in. and twenty $\frac{3}{16}$-in. stropped dead-eyes : an equal number of non-stropped ones is, of course, needed.

Finishing the Dead-eyes.—Before inserting the dead-eyes into their strops their faces should be made convex. The best way to do this is to make a little holder of $\frac{1}{16}$-in. strip to go round the groove, hold them with this in a small hand vice, file and sand-paper them, and finally give a

dull polish with a brass-wire scratch brush. The strops
are painted white, and it is much easier and quicker to
paint them before the dead-eyes are inserted.

The shanks and palms for the dead-eyes are made
next. The shanks are made of brass wire and the palms
of thin copper plate, each $\frac{3}{16}$ in. square. One end of the
brass wire is filed to an angle, and is soldered on to the
centre line of the palm. Two holes are drilled through
each side of the palm and countersunk for the rivet heads.

The dead-eye strops now have to be riveted on to their
corresponding shanks, which are soldered on to the $\frac{3}{16}$-in.
square palms. These rods are cut of such a length that
when the bottom edge of the palm is touching the waterways $\frac{3}{32}$ in. of the shank shall be above the main rail.
I found $\frac{13}{16}$ in. to be the right length. The end $\frac{3}{32}$ in. is
squeezed in a vice to flatten it. In doing this be sure to
flatten the wire at right angles to the palm, otherwise the
dead-eye will be facing in the wrong direction. Drill
each flat to correspond with the holes in the strops, push
one of the small copper nails through, cut off the end, and
rivet it down. For this you want a fine-pointed stake ;
a fine pin-punch does very well. There is just a precaution which might be mentioned here. The strops may
be a fairly tight fit on the dead-eyes, and when riveted
the dead-eye may be quite immovable in the strop, so
see that the bottom hole of the dead-eye is at the bottom,
otherwise you may not be able to move it.

The Dead-eye Plates.—The dead-eye palms are now
riveted to copper plates, which are fixed between the
stanchions. These copper plates are $\frac{3}{8}$ in. wide and
$1\frac{1}{16}$ in. long (v. Fig. 34). Each has three countersunk
holes along the bottom edge through which they are
nailed to the outer edge of the waterways with copper
nails. After nailing, the projecting heads are filed off
flat. The countersink holds them sufficiently. The thickness of the copper plate is the same as that of the straps to

which the bulwark stanchions are fixed. I used this method of riveting the palms to copper plates instead of to the bulwarks direct, as the latter are made of $\frac{1}{32}$-in. ply wood,

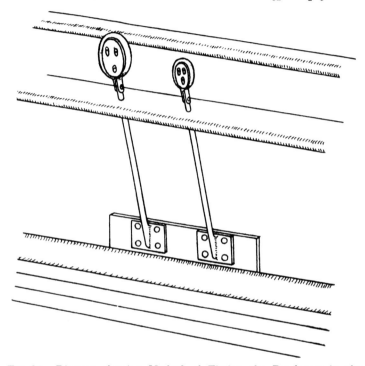

FIG. 34.—Diagram showing Method of Fitting the Dead-eyes in the Model. The strop is riveted to the shank : the lower end of the shank is soldered to a square palm, and the palms are riveted to a plate. The lower edge of this plate is riveted to the outer edge of the waterways. In the drawing there should be a line parallel with the edge of the main rail to show the junction between the main rail and the extra width of pin rail.

and I was afraid that such thin material might not stand the pull of the rigging. In the actual ship the palms are riveted to the bulwark plating.

The position of the dead-eyes in relation to the stanchions must be carefully noted. The first dead-eye in each case is exactly opposite the centre of the mast.

Their positions are shown in the bulwark diagram, which will be found in the folder at the end of this volume.

The length of the rigging along the main rail is—

Fore rigging . . . . $5\frac{3}{8}$ in.
Main rigging . . . . $5\frac{13}{16}$,,
Mizzen rigging . . . . $4\frac{11}{16}$,,

The lower shrouds are $\frac{5}{8}$ in. apart; the topmast and other backstays come at closer intervals. A close inspection of Rennie's sail plan shows a peculiarity. In the case of the fore and main mast the first topgallant backstay comes down to the rail between the fourth and fifth shrouds. This is called a breast backstay. A $\frac{3}{16}$-in. deadeye must therefore be provided for it between these shrouds. There is also a capstay, shackled to eyes on each side of the fore and main mast cap, which is set up to a dead-eye between the first and second topmast backstays. The mizzen has no capstay.

Angularity of Dead-eye Shanks.—Each dead-eye shank should run in the line of the pull of its corresponding shroud or stay. It will be found that the angularity required is very slight, being most marked in the case of the fourth and fifth shrouds.

To find the correct position for riveting the palms to the plates, the best way is to tack the plates to a strip of wood, leaving a $\frac{3}{16}$-in. gap between each plate for the stanchion strap. Six plates are needed on each side for the fore rigging and five for the main rigging. Then you can mark off on each plate the centre line for the various dead-eye shanks and rivet on the palms. The rivet holes at the back or outboard side of each plate should be countersunk. In riveting, the head of the rivet is kept inside, and the end hammered down flat into the countersink. File the back quite smooth afterwards.

Fixing the Stanchions.—When all the stanchions with their butt straps and the dead-eyes with their plates are made, they can be fixed permanently in their proper position between the main rail and the waterways.

Before beginning to fix the stanchions, cut out a small block of wood $1\frac{1}{16}$ in. wide, with square sides, and thick enough to slip easily between the waterways and the main rail ; also half a dozen more thin strips exactly $1\frac{1}{16}$ in. wide. These will act as guides in fixing the butt straps.

Start by laying the copper plates of the dead-eyes flat between their respective butt straps. Their exact position can be taken off the diagram. Aft of these slip the $1\frac{1}{16}$-in. wood strips between the next lot of straps. Cross over to the other side and see if the straps *look* straight. You have got to go by the look of them as much as anything. The straps are at right angles to the deck and not to the horizon, so that their horizon angles are constantly varying. If you get the first lot looking square, and use the strips as gauges, it is moderately easy with care to fix them all satisfactorily.

Screwing the Straps to the Main Rail.—The actual process of fixation is easy. Holding it in a pin vice, put a fine thread on a bit of brass wire by passing it through the No. 9 hole of a jeweller's screw-plate. With the jeweller's drill make an appropriately sized hole through the main rail and the underlying flange of the butt strap. The small rectangular block of wood helps here if it is held up against the side of the strap. The hole need not be tapped, but the threaded wire can be simply screwed in and cut off. It is wise to leave $\frac{1}{4}$ in. projecting until you are quite sure that the positions are true. Afterwards it can be cut and filed off flush with the main rail.

The bottom leg of the strap is fixed to the waterways by a $\frac{3}{16}$-in. copper pin hammered in gently (*v.* Fig. 35). The outer side of the hole in the strap is countersunk, and the head is filed off flush. There is no outward pull on the straps, and the small rivets are quite enough to stand any reasonable upward pull.

The dead-eye plates should be fitted at the same time as the stanchions, but before fixing them, grooves should be cut with a small round file on the inner edge of the main rail into which the shanks fit. Remember that the after dead-eyes are subject to an angular pull from the mast above, and cut the groove accordingly. This angularity is not so great as might be expected, and is most marked in the case of the fourth and fifth lower shrouds. Put up a mast temporarily, and tie a piece of cotton to it at the level of the lower top, the topmast cross-trees, topgallant, and royal mastheads. In this way the angularity of the shrouds and backstays is obtained, and the dead-eye shanks are bent to correspond.

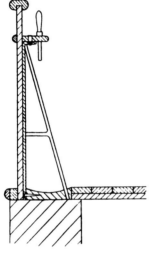

FIG. 35.—Section showing Structure of Bulwarks. The strap is held by a screw passing through the main rail into its flange and at its lower end by a pin driven into the outer edge of the waterways.

If the outer surface of the dead-eye plates does not come flush with that of the butt straps, bend the dead-eye shank slightly so as to tilt the plate inwards or outwards as the case may be.

When all the stanchions and dead-eye plates are fixed, the tops of the screw wires can be cut off and filed flush. Fig. 36 is a photograph showing the construction before the bulwarks have been fixed.

The dead-eyes for the mizzen rigging must be arranged somewhat differently. Instead of being riveted to shanks and plates, each dead-eye is riveted to a short rod on which a $\frac{1}{16}$-in. thread is formed. The main rail is continued aft on to the poop deck, where it becomes the margin plank. Drill holes through this down into the solid wood underneath and screw the dead-eyes in. With a touch of glue on the threads they will hold perfectly. The first shroud for the mizzen mast will come on the main deck and not on the poop deck. To keep it in line with the other mizzen shrouds a hole must be drilled for it in the centre of the main rail. I made a plate and rod for it, and to the end of this rod soldered a short length of $\frac{3}{32}$-in. rod, drilled and threaded $\frac{1}{16}$ in. The first mizzen dead-eye screws into this.

FIG. 36.—The Main Rail, Main Rigging Dead-eyes, and Bulwark Stays before the Bulwark itself has been put on. Note the outer edge of the waterways to which the straps and dead-eye plates are pinned.

Altogether, it will be noticed that a considerable amount of work is necessitated in fixing up the lower dead-eyes.

The upper dead-eyes are, fortunately, less exacting, as they have no strops. There is a little point here which may be mentioned about the upper dead-eyes. The inboard end of the hole through which the lanyard is first passed does not have a score, as the knot butts against it. The method employed for making the lower dead-eyes may be used : as the shrouds are not so wide as the strops, the groove is not so wide, and should be concave in section instead of flat.

CHAPTER IX.

THE BULWARKS—*continued.*

The Pin Rails.—The pin rails must now be made and fixed. Not only do these rails carry the pins, but in the model they have the more important function of keeping the dead-eyes locked in the grooves cut for them in the main rail; it is very important, therefore, that this bit of rail should be securely fixed.

The pin rails are made of teak, $\frac{3}{32}$ in. wide, $\frac{1}{16}$ in. thick. It is quite probable that originally they were sheathed in brass. The fore pin rail extends for $\frac{1}{4}$ in. on the fore and after sides of the fore rigging; the main pin rail extends $\frac{1}{2}$ in. on the fore side and 1 in. on the after side of the main rigging. I have given mine more pins than there are at present on the ship, viz., twenty-five on the fore rail and thirty-seven on the after main rail; the holes are drilled at $\frac{1}{4}$-in. intervals on the fore and $\frac{3}{16}$-in. on the main; to get them evenly spaced they are drilled through the usual little two-holed jig, a pin being stuck through one hole while drilling the next.

The main pin rail runs practically straight, and may be glued and pinned to the main rail, but the fore pin rail has to fit into a slight concavity in the main rail under the fore rigging. To ensure a joint here which will not come unstuck, it is prudent to pin and glue one or two thin strips of boxwood under the two rails transversely.

The layout of the main rigging is shown in Fig. 37,

which was taken on the ship. Fig. 38 is a photograph of the main-rigging dead-eyes in the model.

The dead-eye shanks and plates and the stanchions with their butt straps are oxidised black before being fixed in position.

Belaying Pins.—Altogether there are about a couple

Fig. 37.—The Main Rigging on the Starboard Side, Looking Aft. Note the method of fixing the dead-eye palms to the bulwark. The white double block is for the upper and lower topsail braces.

of hundred belaying pins to make. A pin has a shank about 1 ft. long and a shaped handle about 9 in. long. The model pin, therefore, should be $\frac{7}{16}$ in. long. I made mine in a series of operations.

Operation 1.—Brass wire between $\frac{1}{16}$ and $\frac{3}{64}$ in. in diameter is chosen to make the pins. A length is pulled straight and put in the chuck, leaving $\frac{1}{8}$ in. projecting. A drill chuck holding a No. 9 running-down cutter is put in the tail stock. Start the lathe, and file the projecting wire to a point. Run up the cutter and start the cut. Withdraw the cutter, stop the lathe, open the chuck, and pull out $\frac{3}{8}$ in. of the wire. Start the lathe again and run down $\frac{5}{16}$ in. of the wire. All this performance is unnecessary if you have got straight lengths of wire ; but if your wire is taken off a coil it is very difficult to pull it out straight. This is the reason for leaving only $\frac{1}{8}$ in. projecting when the cut is started, and ensures running down the wire more or less concentrically. Having run down $\frac{5}{16}$ in. of the wire, with a small, smooth file clean up the surface

FIG. 38.—Main Rigging Dead-eyes on Starboard Side of the Model. Two freeing ports are visible, also the rail winch and small bollard on main rail. The two upright columns support the boat skids. The bulwark stanchions and their straps show up dark.

of the cut and take off the burr at the shoulder. Stop the lathe again and pull out about another $\frac{3}{8}$ in. With a pair of cutting pliers snip off the wire, leaving $\frac{1}{8}$ in. projecting as before, and start again.

Operation 2.—In a small piece of scrap wood $\frac{1}{4}$ in. thick, drill a hole of the size of the run-down portion. In another piece, $\frac{3}{16}$ in. thick, drill a hole of the size of the original wire. These two bits of wood are used as jigs to cut the blanks so far made to the same length. To do it accurately, each blank should be held in a pin vice at the shoulder before being pushed into the little jig and clipped off to length. When clipping off the thin end, file the end flat on the jig.

Operation 3.—Put the drill chuck in the head stock ; put a blank in with the unfiled end projecting, file it square, and then round it off.

Operation 4.—Make a small washer about $\frac{1}{32}$ in. thick of hardened steel out of a bit of broken hack saw. Put the run-down part of a blank into the drill chuck, pushing it in up to the shoulder. Slip on the washer, and file a groove with a small triangular file. To get this groove of approximately the same depth in all the pins, count, say, fifteen or twenty strokes of the file, and with a small flat pillar file the handle to shape. By using the washer, a little ring of the wire is left of the original size, and this forms a stop to prevent the pin from slipping through the pin rail. A touch with fine emery cloth will remove any file marks.

Not a very enjoyable job these belaying pins, and at the end of it one thinks it might have been worth while to go to the expense of having a pair of dies cut to squeeze them out. After making, they should be plated and oxidised black.

Scuppers.—The next fittings to make are six little plates which fit over the scupper holes, of which there are three on each side. They are situated as follows :—

The first abreast of the after end of the fore-deck house, the second abreast of the main mast, and the third 6 ft. on the fore side of the after end of the after-deck house. The plates are made of thin copper sheet filed to a flat half-oval shape. A half-circle of thin copper wire is soldered on their face to form a lip, and the plate filed out to fit ; the lower part of the plate fits against the outer edge of the waterways, and is attached by a couple of copper pins. There are also six outside scupper plates with lips formed in the same way. These are attached beneath the lower half-round rubbing strake, with their straight edges up and their half-oval edge down. The inside ones are painted white and the outside ones are oxidised black.

It will be noted that the scuppers are only found about the lowest part of the sheer line ; they are there to drain off any residual water which does not escape through the clearing ports, and after washing down the deck, and so on.

Rail Winches and other Main-rail Fittings.—The rail hand-winches (v. Fig. 39) should now be fixed by glueing and pinning them to the main rail just abaft the

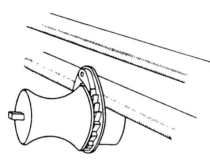

main pin rail. There are only two of these rail winches in the ship at present, but there is some reason to believe that originally there were four, a pair being fixed abaft the fore rigging.

Small eye-bolts for the main and fore lower and top-sail brace blocks are screwed into the rail in the positions indicated in

Fig. 39.—Rail Hand-winch, used for Heaving on various Purchases about the Deck.

the diagram, and holes drilled for their pins about 1½ in. in front. A few extra pin holes are also made forward of the fore pin rail and in the waist. The small bollards are also fixed in their proper positions on the main rail, which is now complete. At this stage the holes for the davits and the boat-skid supports should be drilled in the main rail and the waterways, and these fittings are put in place temporarily to see that they fit all right. The skid supports may be left in position, but it is wiser to unship the davits, as they can very easily be damaged ; small ring-bolts are put in the main rail to take the davit guys.

Shaping the Bulwark.—The bulwark proper is now made.

I made mine of a strip of $\frac{1}{32}$-in. 3-ply wood ; the sheets as sold are 3 ft. square, so it is possible to get a strip which runs from the break of the forecastle to about an inch beyond the break of the poop. This strip is shaped something like a banana, with a convex lower edge and concave upper edge. Its width is not the same all the way along, owing to the slight rise of the bulwarks fore and aft. It takes a bit of time to get these strips of exactly the right curvature, and unless they are right the bulwarks will bulge somewhere and not lie flat against the butt straps as they should. Take a strip about 3 in. wide, hold it up against the hull, and pencil a line along the main-deck line from the inside. It is best to do this before fixing the stanchions, etc. Cut it to this line, and although you may not get it to fit the first time, a little trimming up with a spokeshave and a dreadnought file will after a time give a perfect fit. It is quicker in the long run not to be content with anything but a perfect fit. The after edge is made to fit the edge of the piece of 3-ply which covers the counter ; the forward edge is cut square, and will fit into another piece to be made subsequently for the forecastle bulwarks.

When the lower edge fits the sheer line perfectly, the strip is clipped into position against the main rail. I found a few of those cheap spring clothes-pegs (threepence a dozen from Woolworth's) acted very efficiently for this. Paper clips are also useful for this sort of thing. The top of the bulwark has to be $\frac{5}{16}$ in. above the main rail. Make certain that the bottom edge of the strip is in position, and then scribe a line $\frac{5}{16}$ in. above the main rail. An easy way to do this accurately is to make a small hole in a short strip of wood $\frac{5}{16}$ in. from its lower edge ; put a point of a sharp pencil through the hole, and run it along on the rail inside the bulwark. Take the strip off and pare it down to the line with a spokeshave. After shaping the strip, try it again in position, and be very certain that it will lie easily in its correct attitude without any suspicion of bulging or springing out anywhere.

Openings in the Bulwarks.—Now rub down both sides to a smooth surface and mark out on it the position of—

1. The clearing or freeing ports.
2. The mooring ports.
3. The sheave blocks.
4. The midship bumpkin.
5. The swinging boom goose-neck.
6. The scupper holes.

The Clearing Ports.—First cut out the square holes for the clearing ports. These are 2 ft. 2 in. square, so a full $\frac{1}{2}$-in. hole has to be cut. To get these right and their sides at the correct angles, they must be cut parallel with the stanchions and butt straps. Put the bulwark back in position and run a sharp pencil along the edges of the butt straps, fore and aft of each position where a port is shown in the diagram. The sides of the square ports are cut parallel with these lines. I marked off mine by halving the line between the two scribed lines and scribing a $\frac{1}{2}$-in. circle from this point. The lower edge was arranged so that it would just clear the top edge of the dead-eye plates, as one of the ports comes behind the fore rigging and one behind the main rigging. This edge had to be regarded, and was therefore taken as the datum line for the lower edge of all the ports, although it makes them a little bit higher in the bulwarks than they really are. After scribing the circles, draw the squares, and cut them out with a sharp thin chisel ; do this on a vulcanite cutting-block, so as not to break the outer fibres of the 3-ply. The mooring ports are then cut out, and also the sheave holes for sheet blocks, which are set at an angle.

Painting the Bulwarks.—The strips can now be painted. The whole of the inside is given three or four coats of filler, which is rubbed down wet with wet and dry paper,

and a fine surface is thus obtained. The inside is subsequently painted white, but as it has several projections
which will be put on later, it is perhaps better to cellulose-
spray it. The outside is black. The builder will doubtless have his own idea as to the finish he wants to obtain.
I will only say what I did, which at any rate has the great
merit of being simple, quick, and requiring no special
skill with the paint brush, and I think the result is quite
effective. Give a couple of coats of indian ink—Windsor
& Newton's waterproof brand has plenty of body and
does the work well; it dries in quickly, and after it is
thoroughly dry rub in black Meltonian cream (boot polish).
This gives a nice matt polish; the immediate result is
very satisfactory: whether it will last I cannot say, but it
certainly shows no deterioration of surface or polish several
months after application.

The Swinging Port Lids.—There are now several fittings
to be made for the bulwark strips, and the port lids may
be considered first, as there are a dozen of them to make.
These port lids are fitted on the outside of the bulwarks;
they are hinged at the top so that they will open outwards
and allow the water to escape from the decks; a ring
is riveted on to the lower part of the inner surface, through
which a lashing can be passed to keep the port closed.
These port-lid hinges are a bit too flimsy to make to scale
size and at the same time be capable of their normal
functions. I did a bit of a wangle over them (v. Fig. 40).
On the top corners of each lid a piece of copper shim
$\frac{5}{1000}$ in. thick and a bare $\frac{1}{16}$ in. wide was soldered;
before soldering, the strip of shim was folded round a
wire, and the two legs were put one on each side of the
lid, which was cut out of copper $\frac{9}{16}$ in. square and about
$\frac{1}{64}$ in. thick. Two more pieces were folded up in the same
way. The shim is, however, too delicate to hold a rivet.
The hinge was arranged by bending a copper wire to a
right angle, leaving $\frac{1}{8}$ in. at one end and cut off at an inch.

The long leg was then pushed through one of the ears soldered on to the lid, then through the two folded pieces, and, finally, through the other ear : the whole thing looks like a hinge. The straight end of the wire must then be bent to a right angle close up to the ear. To do this it must be held in a grooved wooden slip in the vice, otherwise the ear will be bent hopelessly out of shape,

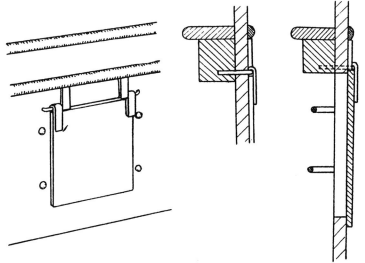

FIG. 40.—These Diagrams show the Method of Fixing the Swinging Lids of the Freeing Ports to the Bulwarks, and the Arrangement of the Dummy Hinges.

and the two right-angled bends must be in the same plane.

The idea is now plain. The ends of the wire are pushed through holes in the bulwarks and the port lid swings on it, the inner folded pieces are dummies, but appear to be supporting the lid ; their upper edges are overlapped and hidden by the upper rubbing strake of half-round moulding. These port lids should lie flush on the bulwark, and in order to get them to do so, after the hinge is made lay the part on a flat bit of steel and press down, with a sharp

edge of a ruler or something similar, the part just below
the ear. The back of the ear then lies flush with the
after surface. I mention this little detail because otherwise the lids will stick out in rather an ungainly fashion.
The lids are painted white inside and black outside, and
the hinges are black.

Fixation Blocks.—Above each port opening a small
block 1 in. long, $\frac{1}{8}$ in square, is glued and pinned inside
the bulwark. This block should fit snugly up against the
lower side of the main rail. It has two functions : first,
the wire of the port-lid hinge is fixed in it, and, secondly,
it is glued and pinned to the main rail and gives, later
on, the permanent upper fixing to the bulwark.

These blocks may be put in position before the inside
painting of the bulwark strip is done, but it is not so easy
to rub it down with these projections. Blocks are also
stuck on for the midship bumpkin and the swinging boom
goose-neck fitting.

The Port Bars.—Then comes another repetition job ;
each port has two port bars horizontally across it to
prevent any movable object from being washed overboard through the ports (v. Fig. 41). I made these bars
of thin copper wire bent over a piece of $\frac{1}{2}$-in square rod.
The ends were bent back parallel with the bar with a pair
of fine pliers, cut off to a gauged length, squeezed flat,
drilled, countersunk, and the little palm rounded off.
These bars are riveted over the inside of the ports. Make
a little jig for drilling the holes for the rivets, so that the
bars shall be evenly spaced in each port. The head of the
little copper rivet is on the outside and the inside end is
cut off short and riveted down into the countersink, the
whole making quite a nice-looking job, and adding one
more to the " shippy " qualities of the model ; altogether,
it need not take more than about three hours to make
and rivet the bars.

Mooring Ports.—There are two pairs in the bulwarks

fore and aft; the diagram of the bulwarks shows their
positions. They are in front of and behind their corresponding bollards respectively. Note that the stanchion
nearest to the hawse hole is bent in to clear the hawser.

The mooring ports in some ships are circular, but in
many, including the *Cutty Sark*, they are oval in shape.
There is an outstanding rounded flange on the outer side
of the bulwarks, and another flange on the inner side

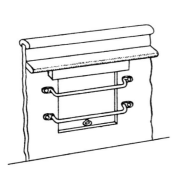

FIG. 41.—Port Lids and Port
Bars seen from inside the
Bulwarks.

FIG. 42—Mooring Ports. They
are made in two pieces with
a push fit, gripping the bulwark between them. The
thicker flange is on the
inside.

which stands out 9 in., supported by webs in the casting.
To make this quite beat me. I had to make them circular,
in two pieces. They are made a tight-push fit to take
the thickness of the bulwarks between the two pieces
(*v*. Fig. 42).

The Bulwark Sheave Blocks.—The only other inside
fittings to make are the four double-sheaved bulwark
blocks. These are 3 ft. 9 in. in length and 6 in. square,
so they may be made of $\frac{1}{8}$-in. square strip $\frac{15}{16}$ in. long. A
strip of $\frac{1}{8}$-in. 3-ply does very well for this and other blocks

in which a sheave is fitted. The middle layer is displaced with the aid of a $\frac{3}{64}$-in. drill and a fine file. The sheaves are turned up of $\frac{3}{16}$-in. vulcanite rod. Note that the sheave pin is not in the middle line of the block ; the edge of the sheave should be level with the outside surface of the bulwark and so the pin must be a little outside the middle line of the sheave block. Remember that the after blocks have a groove cut between the sheaves for

FIG. 43.—Inside of the Bulwarks, showing a Freeing Port, the Sheave Block for the Fore Sheet, and General Structure of the Bulwarks. The large hawser is for mooring purposes.

the after davit. When made, these blocks are also glued and pinned on inside the bulwarks, but if the part is to be sprayed, take the sheaves out and replace them afterwards (v. Fig. 43).

The Scupper Holes.—The only thing that remains to be done before fixing the bulwark in position permanently is to cut a small semicircular notch in the bottom edge over the scupper holes.

Panelling the Bulwarks.—However, I did something else to mine, and that was to panel the bulwarks above the main rail. I made fifty-six little panels, each $\frac{3}{4}$ in. long and $\frac{3}{16}$ in. wide ; they were made of boxwood strip drawn down to a half-round ; the corners were all mitred and glued together in a jig on white paper. They can be seen in Fig. 38. These were glued on to the bulwarks above the rail, and the whole assembly was then sprayed white.

Fixing the Bulwark.—With the blocks above the ports suitably situated, it will be found that the bulwark really holds itself in position very well, but it is a good thing to pin the main rail to the underlying blocks and so get a perfectly secure fixation. The ends of the strip are glued on to the solid sides of the poop and to the solid block which forms the base of the " heads " or men's lavatories at the break of the forecastle. The line of the union between the bulwark and the covering of the counter is hidden by the accommodation-ladder davit on the starboard side, and the eye-plate which holds this can be made with a hole on each side, and small copper nails through each hole make all solid. At the forward end there is, unfortunately, nothing to hide the line, but the plates which carry the three jibboom guy bull's-eyes help to fix the bulwark.

The Forecastle Bulwark.—The bulwark for the forecastle is made next, also of 3-ply, $\frac{1}{32}$ in. thick. The forward edge is cut diagonally to fit into the rabbet cut on the sides of the knightheads ; this piece is about 8 in. long, and its after edge must also be an exact fit with the forward edge of the main bulwark. Cut out a pattern in fairly stiff cardboard to get the shape right. It will be found that it does not fit exactly into the curvature of the margin plank of the forecastle head, and the reason is that the edge of the margin plank is square. Rub down its lower edge carefully and the two will come to a perfect fit. Now cut out the square aperture for the cathead, and drill a small hole on its forward side for the spindle of the anchor release gear.

The **Bill-Board.**—In addition, glue on the bill-board. This is $\frac{3}{4}$ in. wide and $\frac{1}{8}$ in. thick, and long enough to reach from the main-deck level to within $\frac{1}{32}$ in. of the top of the bulwark. I should have mentioned that the top edge of the bulwark is $\frac{5}{16}$ in. above the deck level of the forecastle head, and it is marked out and cut as previously described. The bill-board is a solid plank of timber placed in this position to withstand the assaults of the anchor when it is being got on board, and the bill of the anchor is its most offensive part—hence the name. The lower half-moulding covers its lower edge, but the upper moulding runs underneath it. Cut a groove, therefore, for the moulding to lie in.

Before glueing it in position screw into its front edge, about $\frac{1}{8}$ in. from the bottom, the bull's-eye for the bowsprit shrouds. When we come to the rigging section it will be pointed out that this is the correct spot for the bowsprit shrouds to set up, and it would be found very difficult to screw in this bull's-eye when the bill-board is glued on to the bulwark (*v.* Fig. 12).

Fixing the Forecastle Bulwark.—The top part of the forecastle bulwark is painted white inside and the outside is all black. The bulwark is then glued and pinned in position. It has a tendency to spring outwards at the knightheads : this tendency is counteracted by the $\frac{1}{8}$-in. square packing piece which runs along the bottom of the bulwark ; when the top rails are put on, a cross member is pinned to them just behind the knightheads, but to hold them temporarily make a clip of a bit of scrap with a couple of saw cuts to fit over the top of the bulwark. The cathead is bolted down on deck afterwards. It is important to see that the joint at the after end is neat ; the surface behind must be flat and even to make a good landing for the two pieces of bulwark. As soon as they are in position, put on the jibboom guy bull's-eye plate and screw in the three bull's-eyes just between the upper

and the lower half-round mouldings.   A piece of $\frac{1}{8}$-in.
square strip can be tacked on at the bottom to hold them
while the glue is setting.

The Poop Bulwark.—The bulwark round the poop
comes next.   This is a strip of $\frac{1}{32}$-in. 3-ply $\frac{7}{16}$ in. wide.
It is white inside and black outside.   It is glued and pinned
round the vertical edge of the poop deck, where a landing
has been prepared for it (v. Fig. 10), and meets the top
part of the main bulwark opposite the accommodation
davit.   The joint it makes with the curved sides of
the quarter is covered later by the upper half-round
moulding.

Fixing the Packing Strip.—When the bulwarks are
set in position the $\frac{1}{8}$-in. square packing strip must be
finally glued and pinned against them : this strip forms
the 6-in. ledge all round the ship except under the stern.
It fades away under the counter.   Running forwards it
butts against the after edge of the bill-board and is cut
here, but another piece is continued forwards and runs
on the top of the knees of the head up to the figurehead.

The Half-round Mouldings.—The half-round mouldings
are made in several different ways ; the lower one can be
made solid with the $\frac{1}{8}$-in. square packing strip, but as this
fades away at the counter, I think the better plan is to
make all the mouldings thin, and use the same both for
the upper and the lower rubbing strake.   I made mine
out of a venetian-blind slat, as previously described.   The
circular saw was set to a fine cut and the old edge of the
blind slat cleaned off square ; I then bevelled both edges
with a spokeshave and rubbed it down with sand-paper,
and ran it through the saw again and so obtained several
lengths of $\frac{1}{8}$-in. half-round moulding in a few minutes.
Being thin, it would accommodate itself to the curvature
of the stern without the necessity of steaming it.   The
lower moulding is put on first, starting round the stern on
the flat landing which has been prepared for it.   It is

better not to paint it before putting it on, the reason being that it must run in a fair line and the slightest irregularity will show up much better if it is left in the white. The lower moulding runs over the lower edge of the bill-board. Somewhere about this point there must be a joint, and it is better to leave the front piece for the time until the rails and headwork are fixed.

Fixing the Upper Moulding.—The upper rubbing strake of half-round moulding is now fixed, and it must also be a fair line, running parallel with the lower one, at the level of the main rail; this means the deck-level on the poop and forecastle head. The upper end of the dummy hinges of the port lids are hidden under this rail. One cannot trust to glue alone, it must be pinned as well, and the pins of $\frac{1}{32}$-in. drawn boxwood have to hit off the outer edge of the main rail. I think the best way to do it is to fix it firmly at one end first, and then to glue it in position to get the line fair; clip it with clothes-pegs until set, and then put in pins about every 4 in. or so. The easiest way to get the line fair is to get three or four metal paper-clips, clip them over the bulwarks, with one edge resting on the main rail inside. The outside half of the clip will give the line. Paint the glue on the inside of the mould-ing, fit the after end against the bit coming round the stern, and lay it up to the edge of the clip, fixing it as you go forward with spring clothes-pegs. I found the line came quite fair without any trouble. When the glue is set put in the little dowels.

The Topgallant Rail.—The topgallant rail, sometimes called simply the top rail, sits on the top edge of the bulwark. It is 6 in. wide and 4 in. thick, or in scale size $\frac{1}{8}$ in. by $\frac{1}{16}$ in. full. This rail round the forecastle head is 9 in. wide, the 9 in. fading off into the 6 in. at the break of the forecastle. On the forecastle head and round the poop the rail has to carry metal stanchions, and therefore it must be firmly fixed. The only way to do it is to cut a

groove on its under surface into which the top edge of the
bulwark will fit and can be securely glued.

Grooving the Top Rail.—I made the top rail of beech :
the groove was cut with a makeshift tool, which acted
quite well. A saw cut was made at the end of a piece
of 2-in. by $\frac{1}{2}$-in. scrap. Two strips, $\frac{1}{2}$ in. by $\frac{1}{16}$ in., were
tacked down on each side of the saw cut ; the distance
between them was $\frac{1}{8}$ in., and the saw cut was exactly in
the middle. The sharp corner of a scraper was then
inserted into the saw cut and the 2-in. strip then gripped
in the vice : this held the scraper tight. The $\frac{1}{8}$-in. by
$\frac{1}{16}$-in. beech strips were then drawn through, and the
projecting tooth of the scraper fairly quickly scraped out
a regular and even groove, which fitted on to the top
of the bulwarks quite securely, even without the aid of
glue. The $\frac{3}{16}$-in. pieces for the forecastle were made in
the same way and were subsequently steamed and bent
to shape.

The Top Rail of the Poop.—The real teaser was the
piece which has to fit on the top of the bulwark round
the stern. This is practically a semicircle with about a
4-in. radius. It is difficult to get even a steamed piece to
go round this curve, and as the groove must be ploughed
before the bending, there is some risk of disturbing the
groove. I got over the difficulty by an accident. I was in
the kitchen one day and my eye fell upon a fine sieve. The
top was a wide ring made of beech and a good $\frac{1}{8}$-in. thick,
so I purloined it and cut a half-inch ring off it : a bit of
scrap deal was then screwed on to the face-plate and
turned to a disc. The strip from the sieve was opened
and screwed on to the edge of this disc. It was then a
simple job to face up the edge of the ring, cut a groove
in it, and part off a ring $\frac{1}{16}$ in. thick. This ring was subsequently spread out on a former the shape of the stern,
and the necessary amount cut off its ends to fit round the
bulwark.

Fixing the Top Rail.—The pieces of top rail must then be fitted together. The front end of the forecastle piece is housed in a little slot cut in the knightheads at the top of the bulwark rabbet, and can also be held down by screwing it to the top of the cathead. The rest can be glued in position and thus complete the fashioning of the bulwarks.

Outboard Furnishings of the Bulwarks.—The outside attachments are then pinned on, namely the midship and counter bumpkins, the sockets for the accommodation-ladder davits, the remaining bull's-eyes for the head rigging, and the goose-necks for the swinging boom. These require a small block on the outside of the bulwarks to enable them to clear the upper moulding ; with the block they are able to fold back along the ship's side better.

The bull's-eyes for the bowsprit shrouds should have already been screwed into the fore edge of the bill-board ; the three jibboom guys are set up to bull's-eyes just opposite the break of the forecastle ; the plate for these is fixed about halfway between the two half-round mouldings.

The chain back ropes or goblines are set up to a bull's-eye just below and in front of the cathead. Two bull's-eyes are screwed in above the hawse hole to take the rest of the rigging, which will be described in the second volume of this book.

Eye-bolts are also screwed in below the sheave blocks amidships and at the break of the poop, to which the fore and main sheets are shackled when in use, and there should also be an eye-bolt fairly low down on the hull for the swinging boom martingale block.

The six outside scupper plates can then be nailed on. Another little detail that may be added now that the half-round mouldings are in place is the rudder chain. These chains are shackled to an eye-bolt fixed into the back edge of the rudder just above the copper; they are then carried up together and fixed amidships just above the lower moulding. Each chain then runs along the moulding about as far as the quarter bumpkin. These chains could be used to control the rudder if the ordinary steering gear broke down.

CHAPTER X.

DECK FITTINGS.

Deck Houses.—There are two deck houses, of which the dimensions are :—

Fore-deck house.	Long, 30 ft.	$=7\frac{1}{2}$ in.
	Wide, 10 ft. 9 in.	$=2\frac{11}{16}$ in.
	High, 6 ft. 6 in.	$=1\frac{5}{8}$ in.
After-deck house.	Long, 24 ft.	$=6$ in.
	Wide, 10 ft. 9 in.	$=2\frac{11}{16}$ in.
	High, 6 ft. 6 in.	$=1\frac{5}{8}$ in.

Position of Houses.—To get the correct position of the houses measure off 6 ft. 3 in., or $1\frac{9}{16}$ in. from the back of the foremast to front of fore house, and $4\frac{7}{16}$ in. from the front of the mizzen mast to the after end of the after house.

The plans (*v.* Figs. 44 and 45) show the position of doors and port holes. The houses were divided inside into several compartments, but these need not be shown in the model. The outside of the houses was decorated with moulded panelwork; each panel has a rounded but not semicircular top. At the corners are rounded pillars. The roof has a considerable camber, and projects a little all round. Between the wall of the deck house and the roof is a cornice moulding.

The Carcass.—Make the carcass of the house first of some thin wood, such as $\frac{1}{16}$-in. mahogany. Fit a piece of wood about $\frac{1}{2}$ in. thick inside each end and screw the carcass to these with countersunk $\frac{1}{4}$-in. screws and it will

127

never come apart. The corners must be rabbeted into pillars, which may be made of boxwood. It is easier to round them when built into the house. The panelling and other decorative work take up a considerable time. I did not follow the exact layout of the panels, nor the exact pattern, on account of the technical difficulties, the first of which was making the mouldings small enough, and the second was the shape of the round head of the panels, so I aimed at a panelled effect.

The Mouldings.—To make the mouldings, take a stiff bit of tin-plate, and in the edge cut with a round file two unequally sized round notches running into each other. With this makeshift tool it is possible to scrape down boxwood strips into a moulding, and with a little trouble other patterns of moulding, such as the cornice moulding, can be obtained. For the rounded tops of the panels I made a tube of boxwood of the requisite size in the lathe, moulded the face with the same tool, and parted off rings. These cut in half gave two tops.

Making the Panels.—The panels were put together in a small jig to keep them to the right size : the jig was simply three strips of thin ply wood tacked on a board. A slip of paper was put in the jig, and the semicircular top, side, and bottom member of the panel glued on the paper, the lower joint, of course, being mitred. On pulling out the slip of paper from the jig, the panel mouldings kept their relative position, and could be put aside to dry while others were made. Put a weight on them to keep them flat. When dry, the paper was trimmed round the edges, and the whole thing then glued on to the deck house. They were set in groups of three, as in the real ship, and between each group an upright pilaster of flat $\frac{3}{32}$-in. boxwood was fixed. The doors and panels were made of the same size to obtain a balanced layout of the panelling. The port holes were let in at the top of the panels. The diagram shows their positions. A

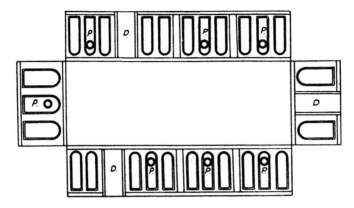

D = DOOR

P = PORT HOLE.

FIG. 44.—The Spread-out Plan of the Fore-deck House. The panelling is shown as carried out in the model. In the ship itself there are more panels and the top arch is flatter. The panels are white and the background is bright work (*i.e.*, teak, varnished).

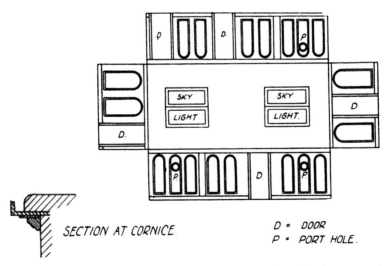

SECTION AT CORNICE.

D = DOOR

P = PORT HOLE.

FIG. 45.—Plan of the After deck House or Half-deck. The galley is at present situated in the fore compartment of this house. Originally it was in the after compartment of the fore house.

three-cornered cornice moulding runs along the top : this
is a bit difficult to fix at the fore and aft ends of the houses
on account of the curve on the upper edge. A moulded
covering board is fixed round the bottom edge. It may
be noted here that it is a good move to make the deck
houses and the hatches before laying the deck. They can
then all be placed in their correct positions and their
mitred deck surrounds cut and laid to them. It is much
more difficult to make the houses, etc., to fit an opening
already made in the deck.

The Roof.—The roof is curved from side to side, and
there is a slight projection for a water drip. They are at
present covered with a kind of tarred roofing felt, but
I have some reason to believe that originally they were
roofed in with teak planking and caulked like the deck.
In order to obtain and keep the camber on the roof, cut
three curved beams for each house and screw a sheet of
$\frac{1}{16}$-in. white sycamore on to them, and plank the top with
$\frac{3}{16}$-in. teak planking. The beams should be a really nice
fit, so that they may keep the sides of the houses from
warping inwards.

A boat was kept on the top of the fore house, upside
down. On the top of the after house there is a skylight
and the galley funnel. The galley is in the fore end of the
after house, but was probably in the after end of the fore
house originally. It has two doors, one in front on the
port side and one in the side of the house on the starboard
side. These doors are in two halves, so that the upper
half could be hooked back while keeping the lower half
shut.

The Boat Skids.—The fore-boat skid crosses the after-
deck house in the position indicated in the diagram of the
bulwark layout, and the accommodation ladder used to
be kept on the top of this house when at sea.

Ladders.—Each deck house had a short ladder at the
fore port corner. They have half-rounded wood uprights

and round metal rungs, four in number, and are therefore very easy to make. Place two pieces of half-round stuff, $\frac{1}{16}$ in. across the flat, together, and drill them for the wire rungs. There is a small handhold on the roof of each deck house above the ladder.

When I built up the deck houses as described I was under the impression that they were originally painted white all over, as they are at present, and I intended to have them cellulose sprayed. However, I learnt later that the original colour scheme of the houses was white panels on a bright varnished background of teak. I tried to get this effect, but found it quite impossible with the panels in position ; so they had to come off, and mostly came to bits in the process, which entailed building them up again. With the panels off it was possible to obtain a uniform background, deep brown in colour and not too shiny, so that it looks very like polished teak. The panels were sprayed white, and glued on again. One can never be quite certain how glue is going to work on a polished surface, therefore it is wise to scratch the surface under each panel to give the glue a key.

The Port Holes.—The port holes were turned out of thick brass tube ; a shoulder was formed inside, against which a $\frac{3}{16}$-in. circular disc of transparent celluloid was fixed instead of glass.

The Doors.—The doors were made of mahogany veneer to give a slight contrast. Each has a turned handle and a pair of dummy hinges, which can be easily bent up, of brass shim round a thin brass wire, and filed off to correct length.

The houses should be an exact fit in their mitred surrounds on the deck, and should " stay put " even without a touch of glue. If, however, you feel doubtful about it, anchor them down to one of the deck beams. I was careful in making the roof of each deck house to secure a really good fit, so that the roof could be lifted off to get at the inside of the ship and would keep in position when replaced.

I arranged the bolt holes in the bottom of the hull to come under the deck houses ; not that it is really necessary, but I always like to know that if I want to get at a thing it is not impossible.

THE BOATS.

There are two lifeboats carried on skids over the after-deck house. At present these skids are over the fore house. They are apparently the original skids, but were placed in this position by the Portuguese owners. The after skid as it is now would get in the way of the main tack.

Position of Boats.—The frontispiece of Lubbock's book and the photograph on p. 248 are very good guides to the ship as she was in Captain Woodget's days. Photographs are not liable to the vagaries of a painter's memory, and both these illustrations show the lifeboats on the skids over the after-deck house, with their davits. An interesting little bit of evidence still survives in the ship regarding the position of these davits. In the main rail aft there is a square repair piece let in just over the double sheave block for the main sheet in the bulwarks. Between the two sheaves there is a vertical groove cut in this block, into which the shaft of the davit was intended to fit, its foot being housed in a step bearing in the waterways. The centre of this sheave block is 13 ft. 9 in. from the break of the poop, and therefore fixes the exact position of the after davit. The fore davit was placed as close up to the main rigging as possible : it could not be mixed up with the main rigging, and its position was therefore determined by the spread of the rigging along the rail. Placing the davits in these positions gives 19 ft. between them.

The after skid is placed so that it just clears the forward edge of the after hatch : the forward skid is 20 ft. forward of it, which brings it to the level of the second topgallant backstay. The photograph of the ship lying in Sydney Harbour, taken broadside on, shows the arrangement clearly.

Construction of the Boats.—The lifeboats were of the double-ended type, and were probably 25 to 26 ft. long and 7 to 8 ft. in beam. Whether they were carvel or clinker-built is uncertain, but for model purposes one is entitled to chose the easier carvel-built boats. These work out at $6\frac{1}{2}$ in. long and $1\frac{7}{8}$ in. wide. They can be carved out of the solid in pine or some other suitable wood. I have found that an easy way to build these boats is to make them in halves, held together by $\frac{1}{8}$-in. dowels at the bows and stern. The outside can be shaped first, and then the two halves are taken apart for hollowing out : one can get at the inside better in this way. Get them as thin as possible. When hollowed, make a saw cut along the keel line, and for the stem and stern posts, which can be let in, and the whole glued together. The boat should now be lined with $\frac{1}{32}$-in. 3-ply. The sides of the well of the boat are vertical and the floor is flat. The seats, five in number, are now put in, and small pieces let in between the seats to form the side seats. Shaped pieces are placed in the bows and stern to complete the seating accommodation and to cover in the air-tight spaces. The inner side of the bulwarks is lined, and a shaped strip forms the gunwale.

Two knees must be placed at the end of each seat, butting against the bulwarks, and shaped knees are fitted into the angle at the bows and stern. A half-round $\frac{1}{16}$-in. rubbing strake is pinned and glued to the outside $\frac{3}{16}$ in. below the gunwale, and the outer edge of the latter is finished off with a half-round moulding of $\frac{1}{32}$-in. boxwood. This completes the woodwork of the boats.

Various metal fittings are required. A ring-bolt is screwed into the angle of the shaped knee at the stem. Larger ring-bolts are placed fore and aft, to which the davit tackles are attached. Metal rowlocks are fitted. A hinged metal housing for the mast is fixed to the front seat, and a square hole in a transverse bar on the floor forms the step for the mast. Two gudgeons for the rudder pintles are screwed into the stern post. Lifelines are looped round each boat. As these lifeboats were meant to sail in an emergency, fittings for the rigging should be present. The rig was generally a simple lug sail. The mast and gaff, with the oars, boathook, etc., would be kept in the boat, but the sail itself would be stowed in a dry place in the ship. Eyes for the shrouds are attached inside the bulwarks, and a couple of cleats for the sheet at the stern. A water breaker is carried in each boat.

The boats are painted white, with a black band between the gunwale and the rubbing strake. To get a first-class finish on these boats paint them over with several coats of filler. The right sort of filler can always be obtained from any firm which does bodywork for motors. It dries very quickly. When you have got a skin of filler on the wood, rub it down with " wet or dry " carborundum paper, wet. This gives a surface like silk, which can either be painted—in which case an amateur will be hard put to it to avoid brush marks—or preferably cellulose sprayed, which gives a perfect finish.

The Gig.—On the fore-deck house a gig is carried, bottom up. It is 5 in. long and $1\frac{5}{8}$ in. in beam ; it has a transom stern. The gunwales of this boat rest in grooves cut in chocks, which are bolted on to the roof of the deck house. Lashings pass over the keel of the boat to ring bolts on the roof. This boat should not be set too far forward on the roof, otherwise its stem will be found chafing the mainstay.

The Boat Skids.—The skids are made of $\frac{1}{8}$-in. square boxwood strip; the fore skid is a little longer than the after one to conform with the shape of the ship. Two longitudinal members are dovetailed in, and pinned for extra security $\frac{1}{4}$ in. outside the outer edge of the after house. On the top of the skids, strips of $\frac{3}{16}$ in. by $\frac{1}{32}$ in. boxwood are pinned and glued and their outer ends are rounded.

The Chocks.—The hinged chocks which carry the boats are very difficult things to make (v. Fig. 46); they ought to be a very close fit to the shape of the boats, and as the skids are sloping outwards and the boats should lie with the stem and stern post vertical, it is quite a problem to cut out these chocks. I made and shaped the outside of the chocks first, cutting them to the usual curvature, and cut

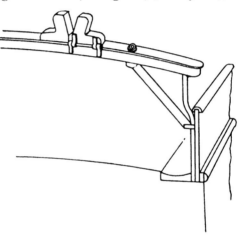

FIG. 46.—Arrangement of Boat-skid Supports and Hinged Chocks.

the base to fit the slope of the skids. I then cut out a V-shaped piece in the centre wide enough to take the boats easily. To get an exact fit the V-shaped gap was lined with a hard-setting moulding paste, and the boats pressed into it. I used Barbola, which is rather sticky, and just wiped the boats with an oily rag, so that after making their impressions they came off easily without pulling the Barbola out. When set hard, the edges can be trimmed and painted. The hinges on the chocks are on their outer halves. The fore chock is supposed to fall forward and the after chock backward.

The Grips.—Grips are provided which hold the boats down on the skids. Each boat has two grips fore and aft. They are pieces of $\frac{1}{16}$ in. by $\frac{1}{32}$ in. brass strip bent at right angles to hold on to the gunwales. The grips are connected to short pieces of chain which end in rings. Ring-bolts are screwed into the skids outside the chocks, and lashings are passed which hold all secure.

Skid Supports.—The ends of the skids are supported on metal pillars, which pass through the main rail and are stepped in the waterways. These pillars have a double-angle bend at their upper ends (Fig. 46). They can be made of $\frac{1}{16}$-in. wire. Angular struts of $\frac{1}{8}$-in. square box-wood runs upwards and inwards from the main rail to the under aspect of the skids. The photograph of the poop on p. 272 of Lubbock's book shows one of these angular struts. It butts against a block fitted to the under side of the skid. These struts require careful cutting to get the angles right ; they should be glued and pinned in position. The after skid, which is not supported, like the fore skid, by the roof of the after-deck house, was provided with a central vertical pillar. This can be made of $\frac{1}{16}$-in. brass wire, provided with a flange at the foot, which fits into a socket in the deck. It is painted white like the rest of the skid assembly.

When drilling the holes for the skid supports and the davits through the rail and into the waterways, it is essential that the holes should tally and be correctly spaced. To do this, lay the whole skid assembly on a piece of paper and mark off the points where the holes should come, and test their accuracy with a pair of dividers. Mark off similar points on the main rail and drill the holes in the rail. Now get a long thin steel rod—a knitting needle will do—with a pointed end. Put this through the hole, and stand away and look at it from the side and from the front of the ship. If you slip one of the masts into its housing you can see at once if the rod is vertical, fore and aft, and the stanchions will give you a guide from the side. The pointed end of the rod can be pressed into the waterways when its position is satisfactory, and the hole is drilled on the mark. I was driven to use this method because I found that, in spite of careful measurement, my first holes did not exactly tally, and it does spoil the look of things if the vertical members are skew-whiff, besides throwing a strain on other parts.

Davits.—Two pairs of davits of the old-fashioned curved-metal pattern are needed for the lifeboats. They are situated close to the boat skids. The shaft of the davit passes through the main rail, and its foot rests in a socket in the waterways. The after davit, it will be remembered, passes through a groove in the block which houses the sheaves in the bulwarks for the mainsheet.

The shape of the davits is well known (*v*. Fig. 47). The usual curvature of the upper part is a quarter of a circle, and this is easy to arrange. Make the davits of $\frac{1}{16}$-in. brass wire. There are two fixtures attached to the shaft : a belaying pin a little above the rail and an

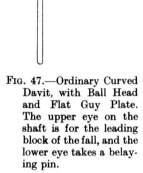

FIG. 47.—Ordinary Curved Davit, with Ball Head and Flat Guy Plate. The upper eye on the shaft is for the leading block of the fall, and the lower eye takes a belaying pin.

eye for attaching a block through which the falls are led. To get a neat and proper hold for these fixtures the wire should be drilled.

Drilling Wire.—As one is often up against the problem of drilling small round stuff it may be useful to describe the method by which it is done. You must make a drilling jig : the time spent on preparing the jig will be amply repaid. Let us take the case of drilling a $\frac{1}{32}$-in. hole through $\frac{1}{16}$-in. brass wire. First take a piece of $\frac{3}{16}$-in. square brass rod. Round this, mark a line with the square, and dot with the centre-punch the centre of the line on two of the surfaces at right angles to each other. Then drill a $\frac{1}{16}$-in. hole through the piece of rod exactly at one of the dots ; through the other dot drill a $\frac{1}{32}$-in. hole, which, if you are accurate, will pass exactly through the centre of the $\frac{1}{16}$-in. hole. All you have to do now is to thread your $\frac{1}{16}$-in. wire through the hole and drill it through the $\frac{1}{32}$-in. hole.

The type of drill stock I fancy for fine work is one used by jewellers for drilling china, and can be obtained from Gray's for 2s. 6d. I discarded the leather thong they supply with it and used a bit of string, which wears out quickly at the hole in the top of the shaft if you do not protect it with a bit of old glove kid, or such-like substance.

You can make your own drills from needles or fine silver-steel wire, or you can buy jewellers' drills cheaply. They are shaped with a spear point ; the thin shanks are very delicate and snap off at the slightest misdirected strain, but otherwise are most satisfactory. Whatever books may say about brass needing no lubricant for drilling, you will find that one of these small drills gets through much more readily if moistened—with anything almost : water, turpentine, paraffin, or " Oilit," the British substitute for the expensive American " Three in One."

In each davit shaft drill two holes in the same direction, one 1 in. and the second $2\frac{3}{4}$ in. from the head. After drilling the holes, the shaft must be tapered at the head. The taper should begin $1\frac{1}{2}$ in. from the head end. This can be done with a file, and you must go easy where the hole is.

The Ball Head.—Next put on the ball head. You can obtain from Gray's $\frac{3}{32}$-in. " gilding metal " beads. They are hollow, made of some bronze-like metal, and have a small hole. Enlarge this hole to take the end of the shaft. Make an eye with a stalk and put it through the upper hole, in the davit shaft, and through the lower hole a belaying-pin holder. Then silver solder the three points.

Drilling Balls.—The next process is to drill the ball head. The tip for drilling balls when they are, as in this case, attached to a rod is to hold the rod in a pin vice with a square nut. The square nut is your guide. Make a small dent in a bit of wood for the ball head to rest in ; have the square nut lying flat, and centre-punch the ball head. Turn the square nut over so that it is lying on its opposite side, and punch again : if you drill the ball from both sides you are certain to get a straight hole. In this case the hole in the head must be drilled at right angles to the holes already drilled in the shaft. This method of drilling balls comes in very useful if you make your own stanchions.

Now make the pins which go through the hole in the ball. In the lathe, file and turn down a scrap of $\frac{1}{16}$-in. wire for $\frac{1}{4}$ in. to something under $\frac{3}{64}$ in. Use a running-down cutter to get a clean shoulder. Cut it off, reverse in the chuck, and file down the head to $\frac{1}{32}$ in. thick. Put the pin through the hole in the head.

Bending the Davits.—The davit is now ready for bending. They must all be bent to the same curvature and at the same spot. The way to do this is to take a $2\frac{1}{2}$-in. diameter round rod of wood, such as an old curtain pole. On the squared face of this mark off the diameter. On the rounded surface at one end of the diameter make a small hole to take the pin of the davit head, and counter-sink this hole slightly (v. Fig. 48). Press the pin and ball in the hole, and with your fingers bend the tapered portion of the davit round the rod until the shaft is parallel with the diameter marked. The head pin will then be parallel with the shaft, and the radius of the curvature is $1\frac{1}{4}$ in., or

5 ft. in the ship. By bending the davits in this way you secure a curvature that is uniform. Note that you should not attempt the bending before soldering in the upper eye, otherwise you are liable to get a kink or a break where the hole has been drilled.

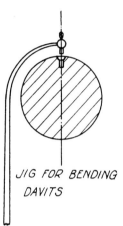

JIG FOR BENDING DAVITS

FIG. 48.—Davits can be correctly Bent by the Simple Jig shown. If the centre line of the ball head is an inch outside the shaft, the davit should be bent round a circular block 2 in. in diameter. The recess holds the pin and ball head steady while the davit is being bent.

The guy plate is now made from a bit of brass. It has a central hole large enough to admit the pin, and a small hole in each side for the guy shackle. The guy plate goes on the top of the ball head. Thread the pin through both, and then flatten that part of the pin which lies beneath the ball by squeezing it in the vice. File to shape, and drill it, which completes the davit. They are painted white.

Accommodation-ladder Davit.— There is a simple smaller davit for the accommodation ladder on the starboard side just abaft the break of the poop. It is stepped outside the bulwarks in a socket resting on the lower moulding. It does not have guy plates or an eye for a leading block, as the fall from the double block at the head is carried straight inboard abaft the third mizzen shroud and belays to the pin rail.

I found this davit useful for covering up the joint between the main-deck bulwarks and the covering of the counter. There must inevitably be a joint about here, and if you arrange the joint between the two parts to come immediately behind the accommodation-ladder davit it will not be conspicuous.

CARGO WINCH.

Between the main mast and the main hatch there is a cargo winch worked by hand. It is rather like the domestic mangle. There are two wooden rollers, one thick and the other thin, but they do not touch each other. At the ends of the wooden rollers are cut gear wheels, and a pawl engaging in the top wheel. The thin upper roller has a squared end on the spindle, to which the crank handle is attached. When light loads were raised from the hold, the rope was turned round the upper roller, but for heavier weights the gearing gave greater power to the lower roller.

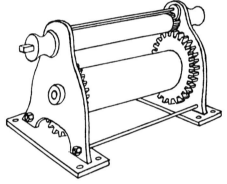

FIG. 49.—Simplified Form of Cargo Winch as Constructed for the Model.

Making the Winch. —The construction of the winch is a simple matter. The two standards are cut from copper or brass plate to the shape shown in the sketch (v. Fig. 49). The feet can be soldered on. Two rods brace the standards together below and one above. Make the wooden rollers, and put the gears on before drilling the holes in the standards for the spindles of the rollers, and then you can be sure that the gears will mesh. The upper gear is a bit of 12-leaf $\frac{3}{16}$-in. pinion wire—obtainable from George Adams—and the lower gear is a $\frac{5}{8}$-in. brass disc, cut with forty-eight teeth, giving a 4 to 1 ratio. It makes a nicer job if small brass bushes are soldered into the standards for the spindles of the rollers. A pawl is fixed to the top bar to engage with the small pinion. The diameters of the roller are $\frac{3}{8}$ in. for the larger one and $\frac{5}{32}$ in. for the smaller. The centre height is 3 ft. 6 in., making $\frac{7}{8}$ in. to the centre of the small roller from the deck. Outside the standards a small boxwood drum is threaded on the shaft on each side. This was used at times for heaving on various purchases connected with the rigging.

Squaring the End of a Shaft.—The shaft has a squared end for the winch handle. If you want to make a squared end to a small shaft for a job like this, the easiest way is to solder on a bit of $\frac{1}{16}$-in. square brass wire. The upper shaft in this little winch is a deception, as it does not run right through the upper $\frac{5}{32}$-in. wood roller. The roller was put in the chuck, carefully centred, drilled, and tapped $\frac{1}{16}$ in. Then a piece of $\frac{1}{16}$-in. wire was threaded, $\frac{1}{16}$ in. for $\frac{1}{4}$ in., and cut off and faced flat $\frac{5}{16}$ in. beyond the thread. The square end was soldered on to this. The shaft was then driven through the boxwood drum, pushed through the bush in the standard, and through the pinion.

Before assembling the parts, cut a small notch in the shaft and in the edge of the hole through the pinion : arrange these notches so that they will come together, and when assembled put in a spot of Britinol paste. A whiff with the blow-pipe on the threaded end of the shaft will make it run, and the solder key so formed is strong enough to hold the pinion on the shaft, which is then screwed into the wooden roller. The other end is treated in the same way, except that there is no need to make the key ; indeed, it is better not to have the other pinion fixed to the shaft, as it will mesh more easily with its gear wheel on the large roller if it runs free. Of course this is not an engineering job, but it looks like the real thing and can be turned round.

Elaborated Winch.—I have reason to believe that a cargo winch was also carried just abaft the fore hatch.

Although the cargo winch described above is a simplified form of the real article, it makes a reasonable scale fitting. For the sake of others who may be inclined to produce a more elaborate winch, I have included one of Mr Denny's drawings (*v.* Fig. 50) which shows the construction.

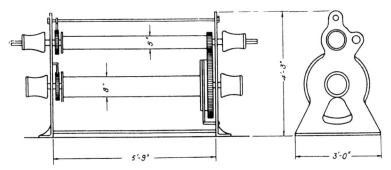

FIG. 50.—Drawing, with Main Dimensions, of the Cargo Winch in the Ship, with Two Wooden Rollers.

THE PUMPS.

Position of Pumps.—The pumps are situated immediately behind the main mast, the conventional position. Every ship leaks a little, and the bilge water thus collected runs to the well amidships; all the timbers or frames of a ship have holes, called limber holes, close to the keel end of the frames, so that water can pass along from any point in the hull to the well. It is, of course, only common-sense to place the pumps at the lowest point of the sheer: firstly, because the lift of the water is less; and secondly, because when discharged on deck it can easily find its way to the scuppers.

Whether the pumps are original or not I do not know. They are unusual in that instead of the ordinary double-throw pump with two pistons, etc., they have three pistons and three wells.

General Design of the Pumps.—The fly-wheels are 4 ft. in diameter, and when viewed from the side just overlap the main mast. The centre of the bearings is 3 ft. 6 in. above the deck, and the overall width is 6 ft. The cast-iron pump wells project 18 in. above the deck and are a foot in diameter. There are three of these wells lying in a line athwartships, and each has a valve pot

Fig. 51.—The Pumps, taken on the Ship from Aft. Note the foot of the main mast and the method of setting up the mizzen stays, also the boat skid and the main fife rail.

cast integrally with it on the after side (*v.* Fig. 51). The valves are rubber discs. The water is discharged from these pots by wide mouths a few inches below the top rim of the pots. The crankshaft is a triple throw shaft with the cranks set at 120° angles. The throw is 6 in., giving an up-and-down motion to the piston of a foot. The pump wells are connected with the bilge well in the hold of the ship by pipes, through which the bilge is sucked up.

Action of the Pumps.—On the upward suction stroke of the pump, the rubber disc valve in the valve pot closes on its seating, and the water is sucked up into the pump well. On the downward stroke a valve at the bottom of the pump well closes, the disc valve in the valve pots opens and the water is forced into the valve pot from which it overflows on to the deck. Provided that the suction rose in the bilge well is kept clean there is very little to get out of order.

The pumps are still used, and Mr Gilbert tells me that about half an hour's pumping twice a week is all the ship needs to keep her clear, which is rather wonderful for a ship of her age.

To make a working model of the pumps is quite possible. Anyhow, the model should be made so that the wheels can be turned, actuating the reciprocating motion, even if the valves and pipe connections are omitted. It would take up too much space to give a detailed description of the whole job, and I must therefore only give a condensed account.

The Pump Wells.—Start by making the pump wells. They are 1-in. long pieces of $\frac{1}{4}$-in. outside diameter copper tube. A brass rim is soldered on to the top with a small square piece on the forward side. The guide for the piston-rod is screwed on to this square. To the after side is soldered the valve pot of $\frac{3}{16}$-in. copper tube.

The base plate, which is at present covered by the deck sheathing in the ship, is made of thin copper sheet with three holes of $\frac{1}{4}$-in. diameter at $\frac{5}{16}$-in. centres. Make a similar plate of $\frac{1}{4}$-in. boxwood to go under the deck, and thus provide a rigid housing for the pump wells. The copper plate must be wide enough to afford a seating for the standards, which consist of two thin copper plates cut to the shape shown in the photographs and soldered together. On the top of the standards there are plummer-block bearings for the crankshaft.

The Pistons.—The pistons are turned from $\frac{3}{16}$-in. brass rod, a loose fit in the tubes. A lug is filed on the top of each piston. On the top of this lug a small hole is drilled centrally, and the piston-rod, which acts as a guide-rod, is soldered in. Another hole is drilled through the lug transversely to take the connecting-rod pin.

A $\frac{3}{64}$-in. hole is then drilled in the square on the forward part of the rim of the pump well, tapped $\frac{1}{16}$ in., and a small $\frac{1}{16}$-in. screw is made to fit it. The guide is a piece of $\frac{1}{16}$-in. brass strip, attached by this screw to the square, and projects over the mouth of the well. A hole is drilled in it through which the guide-rod can slide up and down and so keep the piston itself from tilting and binding in the pump well.

The Connecting-rods.—The connecting-rods are forked, made of $\frac{1}{16}$-in. half-round brass wire bent round in the shape of a hairpin. A hole is drilled and tapped, No. 9 on jeweller's screw plate, at the summit of the bend, and two other holes are drilled at the extremities of the arm of the fork. Thread one of these holes. Fit the fork on to the lug at the top of the piston and screw them together with a pin, making them a loose fit. The guide-rod must be cut short enough to clear the top of the fork inside.

The Big Ends.—The big ends are made next, and it is impossible to make them without a jeweller's screw plate and taps. They are made of $\frac{1}{16}$-in. brass strip and $\frac{1}{16}$-in. square brass wire. A hole is drilled and tapped on the bottom side of them for the straight part of the connection-rod. I need hardly go into the details of making these.

The Crankshaft.—The crankshaft is the crux of the question. In the ship the shaft is bent up of steel rod about 2 in. in diameter. One might model this in five minutes if one spent about a couple of days making a jig to do it in. Instead, I made the crankshaft with square webs. There is no real difficulty if you set about it in the right way. The most essential thing is to have a drill of exactly the same size as that of the wire you are going to use.

The Crank Webs.—The crank webs are made first, six in number, of $\frac{1}{16}$-in. brass strip. Each web has two holes $\frac{1}{8}$ in. apart. The only way to get these holes exactly spaced and central on the strip is to drill them through the simple little two-hole jig. When the webs are all drilled, pass wire through the holes, file one end of the webs square and the other curved.

Now take two pieces of tin-plate 1 in. square; scribe lines at right angles through the centre, make a centre dot, and scribe a circle at $\frac{1}{8}$-in. radius. Dot points at 120° on the circumference of this circle so that the dots on the two plates correspond. Drill holes at these points and at the centre dot. The wire and webs are now threaded together and set up with the help of these plates. Set the webs to a gauge so that they shall be the same distance apart, and remember that you have set the pump wells at $\frac{5}{16}$-in. centres: if the webs are correctly gauged the crankshaft will fit all right.

Soldering the Crankshaft.—Now silver solder the whole thing together. Aim at getting the solder to form a shoulder; firstly, where the crankpins join the inner side of the webs; and secondly, where the main shaft joins the outer side of the webs. This can be done by putting the solder at these points before heating up. Be careful not to overheat or the wire may bend, and be particularly careful to see that everything is perfectly clean beforehand and the boron compound fresh. After pickling, cut off the redundant ends of wire. A hint here: do not attempt to cut out the bit of main shaft inside the webs with nippers; the shaft will almost certainly bend if you do, so it must be filed out.

The Wheels.—The wheels are now made. I have left these to the last, as they are a real treat to make, and when you have made them you will want to carry them

about in your waistcoat pocket to show your friends. I
may say I spent some unhappy hours before I succeeded
in getting them right, but after several failures I found
an easy method of making them, and a method which can
be relied upon to give the result.

Making the Rims.—The wheels are 4 in. in diameter.
The rim is heavy and of rounded section. There are six
spokes, and they are staggered—or curved—that is where
the catch comes in. Each spoke has a flattened ball
threaded on it where it joins the hub. Select the wire you
are going to use for the spokes, and a drill to match.
Soften the wire by heating it. Make the rim first. Face
up a short length of 1-in. diameter brass rod, holding it in
a three-jaw chuck. If you have no dividing plate, make
three dots on the face at the three jaws. With a centre
square, scribe three diameters from these dots and mark
off corresponding lines on the circumference of the rod.
Then with the mop callipers scribe a line round the circumference of the rod and you have your drilling points
for the spokes set out. Drill the six holes in a V-block,
so that you can see the scribed lines on the face, and drill
the holes $\frac{3}{32}$-in. deep, perpendicular to the surface. After
this, turn up the rim in the ordinary way ; you may want
a wooden mandrel for cleaning up the reverse face.

Making the Hubs.—The hub is then drilled for the
spokes. The easiest way to do this is to use a bit of
hexagon rod, say $\frac{3}{16}$ in., across the flats. Each hole can
then be drilled at the centre of a flat. The holes should
meet and be cleared right through. The rod is then faced
and turned circular, about $\frac{1}{8}$ in. in diameter, for $\frac{1}{4}$ in.
Part off $\frac{1}{4}$ in. farther down, leaving a hexagon stump.
Now for the balls. They are purely decorative, but as they
can be put on without much trouble it is worth while to
include them. I have searched all over Clerkenwell for
small brass balls without success. These are hollow metal
—? phosphor bronze—balls, called gilding metal beads,

the smallest of which is about $\frac{3}{32}$ in. There are also small silver hollow balls, down to the size of seed pearls, but they melt very easily and cannot safely be silver soldered. For these wheels I used silver beads rather under $\frac{1}{16}$ in., drilled and threaded on the spokes, and fixed with soft solder.

Assembling the Wheels.—The wheels can now be assembled and soldered together. Take off the three-jaw chuck and have it standing on your work-bench as a vice. Chuck the hub by the hexagon stump, and fill all the drill holes with boron compound. Thread a piece of the spoke wire : first through the rim, then a bead, then right through the hub, a second bead, and, lastly, through the opposite side of the rim. This piece of wire will make two spokes. The four other spokes are then put in position, each with a bead. Make sure that the spokes are firmly lodged in their holes in the hub as deeply as they will go. When all are in position the wheel can be adjusted for symmetry. Leave at least $\frac{1}{8}$ in. of the spoke wire projecting beyond the rim, and move the silver balls so that they are touching the rim and are out of the way of the flame. Now put silver solder on each spoke at the hub end, remove the wheel from the chuck to a handy bit of asbestos gas-fire radiant, and heat up. Direct the flame on the hub. If you have not left too long a stump it will heat up quickly, and all the solder will run nicely without damaging the balls. Pickle, dry, and scratch-brush, and, I might say, prepare to stagger. I spent hour after exasperating hour in preparing jigs and other futile gadgets to try to make staggered spokes separately, and the whole thing can be done in a couple of minutes and very much better.

Staggering the Spokes.—Fix the stump in the chuck again with the rim of the wheel on the surface of the jaws. By comparing the rim with the jaws you can see at once if the wheel is out of truth. Push the balls down the spokes to the hub. Now turn the rim clockwise through

an angle of about 30° ; owing to the softness of the spokes,
and to the fact that they are not fixed to the rim but
only threaded through it, you can turn the rim quite
easily. Adjust again for symmetry. Give the curvature

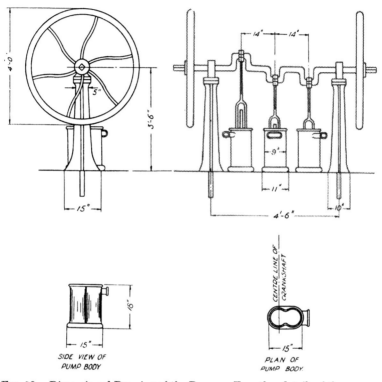

FIG. 52.—Dimensioned Drawing of the Pumps. For other details of the pumps
see the photographs of the foot of the main mast.

to the spokes with a pair of round-nosed pliers. Holding
the pliers vertically, put one nose against the spoke just
outside the ball and the other nose on the opposite side
of the spoke close to the rim. A slight turn of the wrist
and the spoke comes beautifully to the desired shape
as easily as possible. Any projection of the spoke now
left on the rim can be nipped off, touched with soft solder,

smoothed down, and polished. The balls will " stay put " owing to the curvature of the spoke.

The hexagon stump again comes in useful in drilling the hub. It should be drilled for the crankshaft $\frac{5}{32}$ in. deep. The outer $\frac{1}{16}$ in. is opened out to $\frac{3}{64}$ in. and tapped $\frac{1}{16}$ in. The hub can then be parted off. Turn down a short length of $\frac{1}{16}$-in. square rod and tap it $\frac{1}{16}$ in. for $\frac{1}{16}$ in. Screw this into the hub, and holding it by this, face up the reverse face of the hub. Remove and cut off the square rod, leaving $\frac{3}{32}$ in., on to which the pump handle is fitted.

The parts can then be plated and oxidised. I left the crankshaft bright, as it is a nice little job. The spokes of the wheels are painted green. The pump can then be assembled. I found the crankshaft fitted into the hub closely enough to work the pump without any grub screw, and so I left it at that.

A working drawing of the actual pumps is given (v. Fig. 52). This drawing was made by Mr Denny, and gives the exact details and dimensions of the pumps.

THE LADDERS.

There are three ladders, two leading from the deck to the poop and one to the forecastle head. They are all of the same size, and each has four treads. Ladders are very difficult things to make, and after some trial I developed a method of making them which can be absolutely relied upon to give a satisfactory result with the greatest ease. The treads must be housed in slots in the side pieces to make the ladder a sound job, and the slots must be cut (1) the same distance apart, (2) at the same angle, and (3) to the same depth, and without going through the side pieces.

Marking off the Styles.—Say the ladder is to have

treads at 9-in. centres, and the style or side pieces of the
ladder are to be 9 in. wide. First, prepare the styles $\frac{3}{16}$ in.
wide by, say, $\frac{1}{16}$-in. bare. This $\frac{1}{16}$ in. is not scale size, but
it is difficult to do the job with stuff much thinner than
$\frac{1}{16}$ in. Mark off a centre line down the $\frac{3}{16}$-in. strips, and
then with a pair of dividers mark it off with a dot at every
$\frac{3}{16}$ in.

Jig for Slotting the Styles.—A sawing jig must now
be made. Take two old hack-saw blades—which should

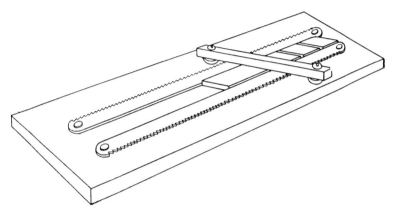

Fig. 53.—Jig for cutting the Slots in Side Members of Ladders. After cutting
the slots in one member the square rod is unscrewed at one end and
swung to the other side, the angle being taken by a bevel.

be of the same thickness—screw them down to a bit of
board with the smooth edges inwards to each other and at
such a distance apart that the $\frac{3}{16}$-in. strip can just slide
between them (v. Fig. 53). Bore at the ends of a 3-in.
length of $\frac{1}{4}$-in. square brass or steel rod two holes big
enough to take a couple of $\frac{5}{8}$-in. screws. Set your
carpenter's bevel to the angle you are going to cut the
slots and screw down the 3-in. rod across the hack-saw
blades at this angle. It is necessary to put a small washer
under each end to allow the $\frac{3}{16}$-in. strip to slide under the
rod, but arrange it so that the strip only just slides under.

Now push the $\frac{3}{16}$-in. strip in until the first dot just shows. I have a fine jeweller's hack saw which I use for this job. Keep the blade hard up against the 3-in. rod and you can go on sawing. You cannot saw too deep because of the hack-saw blades. When one slot is cut, with a light hammer tap up the strip until the next dot appears, and saw again until all the slots are cut.

For the other style of the ladder the 3-in. guide-rod has to be swung over. Take out the upper screw, and with the bevel get it to the same angle on the other side of a line at right angles to the hack-saw blades. Then proceed to saw the slots in the same way. When the two strips are laid side by side, the slots should show a regular V-shaped pattern.

This is one of the jobs where it pays to spend a little time in making a jig, and in this case the jig is a very simple affair, and need not take more than a few minutes to put together.

The Treads.—The treads are the width of the ladder less the thickness of one style : as the ladders are 2 ft. 6 in. wide, the treads should be $\frac{9}{16}$ in. I had some boxwood strip, $\frac{3}{16}$ in. by $\frac{1}{32}$ in., about, which I found satisfactory. Here, again, to get all the treads cut square and of the same length, use a jig. It seems almost unnecessary to describe such a simple affair, but perhaps some of my readers would prefer to have nothing left to their imaginations. In a $\frac{1}{4}$-in. square piece of strip wood cut or file at right angles a groove which will just take the strip you are using for the treads. Screw this, with the groove facing down, on a bit of scrap. Screw a stop at $\frac{9}{16}$ in., plus the thickness of the saw you intend to use. Push the strips through the groove up to the stop and saw off as many treads as you require.

If you prepare the material in this way you can make the three ladders in a very short time. Cut off lengths of the slotted strip by sawing right through the styles at the slots, leaving four whole slots. Put a touch of glue in the slots and fit in the treads, then give the whole thing a slight squeeze, and leave it to set. The accommodation ladder is made in the same way.

SMALL DECK FITTINGS.

Hen Coops.—There are a couple of hen coops at the break of the poop lashed to ring-bolts in the deck on either side of the mizzen mast. These are easily made and need no description.

Spare Spars.—At least a couple of spare spars were always carried. They should be big, and long enough to make a new topmast ; make them octagonal in shape with a square foot. They are lashed to chocks. A pin passed through the centre of the chock holds them on the deck. These chocks will hide a screw if the deck wants holding down amidships.

Bitts or Bollards.—These are perhaps the simplest things to make (*v.* Fig. 54). The base is made of brass strip $\frac{1}{4}$ in. wide and $\frac{3}{4}$ in. long. At $\frac{3}{16}$ in. from each end drill a $\frac{1}{8}$-in. hole, and round the corners. Small holes can be drilled at the corners for the holding-down bolts. Chuck a piece of $\frac{1}{4}$-in. brass rod, turn it down to $\frac{1}{8}$ in. for $\frac{1}{8}$ in. length, then to $\frac{3}{16}$ in. for $\frac{1}{4}$ in., and part it off $\frac{1}{16}$ in. beyond. Reverse and chamfer edges of this $\frac{1}{16}$ in. to a rounded outline. Two of these pieces are needed for each bollard ; they can be pressed into the base if made a tight fit, otherwise solder them in and file the bottom flat. Two pairs are needed on the main deck. In my case they hide the screws holding down the deck. Another pair is found on the forecastle head and a small pair on the poop.

Main-rail Bollards.—Two pairs of very small bollards are mounted on the pin rail at the after end of the fore and main rigging. These were used for belaying the fore and main sheet, which was a big 4-in. rope, and rather too heavy for an ordinary belaying pin. These smallest ones are $\frac{1}{8}$ in. in diameter at the top and $\frac{3}{16}$ in. high (v. Fig. 55).

Fairleads.—On the forecastle head there is a pair of roller fairleads (v. Fig. 56). They can be filed from brass ; an easier way to make a clean job of them is to machine them. Mill out a $\frac{1}{8}$-in. slot for the under surface of the palms and turn the outer and upper face. The centre of the top bar is then cut out and the inner ends of the palms rounded off ; the piece can then be soldered to its base. The central roller is made separately. Take off any sharp edges with a fine file and emery cloth. If you file them from the solid, mark out the centre line and drill hole for centre roller, and then at right angles drill two $\frac{7}{64}$-in. holes equidistant from centre line for the concavity under the palms.

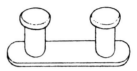

FIG. 54.—Large Main-deck Bollard.

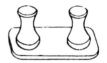

FIG. 55.—Small Bollards on the Main Rail, round which the Sheets or Tacks of the Fore and Main Sail were made fast.

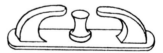

FIG. 56.—A Fairlead with a Central Roller.

Ring-bolts.—A ring-bolt consists of a square or rounded plate which seats on the deck, through the centre of which passes a shank, nutted under the deck, with an eye on the top of the plate ; a ring is attached to this eye, generally circular but sometimes oval in shape. The square plate should be made $\frac{1}{8}$ in. across, and the eye and ring in proportion. Two of these ring-bolts are found on each side of the hatchways. They were used to attach heavy chains and beams, which were placed over the hatchways when bad weather was anticipated. It was extremely dangerous

for a sailing ship to have her hatches stove in, because a
sailing ship was not built, like a steamer, with several
holds separated by watertight bulkheads.   There was
one big hold running practically the whole length of the
ship.   If one hatchway were burst in by the sea, there
was nothing to prevent flooding of the whole ship.   This
was partly the reason why the hatchways in sailing ships
were comparatively small.

Uses of Ring-bolts.—Ring-bolts were also used for
holding down some of the gear : the anchors on the fore
deck have a pair on each side ; the spare spars along
the waterways were lashed down on chocks to ring-bolts ;
the hen coops at the break of the poop and the harness
casks on the poop also have them, so that altogether you
want a considerable number.

Some of the rigging was also fixed to ring-bolts in the
waterways, such as the topsail and other halliards and
the main tack, but these will be mentioned under their
appropriate sections.

Making Ring-bolts.—As several of these ring-bolts
are required, it is well to develop some definite method
of making them.   Each consists of three parts : the plate,
the shank, and the ring, round or oval.   The plates, if
square, are cut off $\frac{1}{8}$-in. brass strip.   They must have the
edges filed square.   To do this, slip the strip into a small
square machine vice, with the edge just projecting.   File
it square ; loosen the screw, push the strip on just over
$\frac{1}{8}$ in.—using a gauge—and cut off with a pair of sharp-
cutting nippers.   File the remaining edge square, and
push out again until you have got the number of squares
you need.   Each square must be put in the vice again and
have the fourth edge filed.   They must then be centre-
punched.   It saves time to use one tool on the lot and to
punch all the plates before drilling any of them.   Your
eye is a good enough judge for the centre point of such
a small square.   Then they must be drilled.   Use the

jeweller's drill, and you will find it useful to keep the square against an edge to prevent it from twisting round as the drill rotates. The small hole is then tapped with a No. 9 jeweller's tap.

The shank is next made : choose a brass wire which will suit the No. 9 hole of the jeweller's screw plate. Thread about $\frac{1}{8}$ in. ; cut off $\frac{1}{16}$ in. beyond the thread. The unthreaded portion is then squeezed flat in a vice, a hole is drilled through it, and the end neatly rounded off. The shank is then screwed into the plate and the ring put in.

If oval rings are required, the easiest way is to take them off an oval linked chain of suitable size. Round rings can be made by winding wire round a round rod and sawing or cutting through the lot together, not a very satisfactory method with very small rings. Gray's, of Clerkenwell, stock what are called jump rings by jewellers. These can be obtained rather under $\frac{1}{8}$ in. in diameter and cost a few pence per gross. It is useful to keep a box of various sizes of these jump rings. After assembly the ring-bolt can be plated and oxidised.

Wood-screw Ring-bolt.—I made a special form of ring-bolt for holding down the waterways (v. Fig. 27). A small brass plate was silver soldered into the slot of a $\frac{1}{4}$-in. brass wood screw. This plate was drilled in the centre and shaped to a half oval, and the ring threaded through. These ring-bolts have all the holding qualities but none of the appearance of a wood screw. They were used in the waterways for the halliard gear, the main tack, etc.

The Fife Rails.—At the bottom of each mast there was generally a three-sided square rail supported on turned solid legs : this rail carried numerous belaying pins for turning up the running rigging. Three of the, possibly, original fife rails remain in the ship, but I have not been able to find out whether she carried more when she began her career. These rails are not of the ordinary three-sided square pattern. They are curved rails, supported on standards, one in front of the main mast, one in front and one behind the foremast—the mizzen mast does not possess one at all. The rail is 6 ft. long, 4½ in. thick, and 1 ft. wide, with holes for four belaying pins in each. It

FIG. 57.—Foot of the Foremast. The old fife rails stepped in solid cast-iron feet are shown well. Note the deck lugs for the mainstays, which are cased in leather where they cross the mast. Note also the method of turning the fore shrouds round the dead-eyes, and compare this with the photograph of the main rigging where the upper dead-eyes are metal stropped. The single block shackled to the lower mast band is the lower block of the fore yard lift purchase.

is probable that more than one rope was turned up on each pin. The supports pass through the rail and their projecting heads are shaped to allow the rigging to be turned up round them. The photographs (v. Figs. 51 and 57) show the main-mast and foremast fife rails very plainly as they are at present. The massive supports are

7 in. thick and 14 in. wide. In the lower third are three sheaves, representing the old-fashioned nine-pin blocks : a purchase could be rove through one of these sheaves and then more room be gained for the crew to heave on it.

The fife rail abaft the foremast is of a slightly different pattern to the two other ones. It is supported on two very solid turned legs, with a single sheave in the bulbous

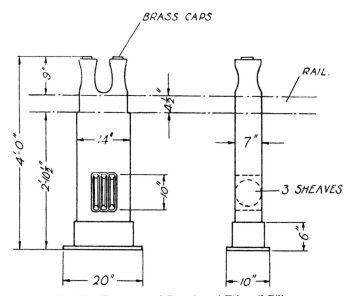

FIG. 58.—Dimensioned Drawing of Fife-rail Pillars.

portion of the leg. These supports are made of wood. A dimensioned drawing by Mr Denny of these supports is given in Figs. 58 and 59. They are all housed in a solid cast-iron socket bolted to the deck.

These rails lend themselves to reproduction in miniature. The rail itself can be made of boxwood or teak, and also the supports. Two of the legs must be turned up and have slots drilled and filed out for the sheaves. The other supports are just over $\frac{1}{4}$ in. wide by $\frac{1}{8}$ in. full thick. The height from the deck to the top of the rail is

3 ft. 3 in., or $\frac{13}{16}$ in.   Boxwood is the best wood to cut them
from, as each must have three slots cut for the sheaves.
The socket can either be filed down from solid, but are
much more easily built up.   Fold a $\frac{5}{32}$-in. wide strip of
brass or copper round one of the supports and hard solder
the junction, and then solder this to a base plate.   The
wooden heads of the supports which project through the
rail can be put on separately.   The edges of the rail must
be rounded to prevent chafing of the gear. The rail itself
is left in the natural colour, and the rest of the fittings
are black. Figs. 60 and 61 show the fife rails on the fore
and after sides of foremast, as made for the model.

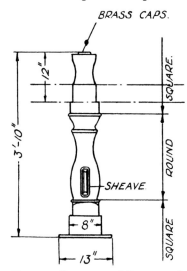

FIG. 59.—Dimensioned Drawing of Turned Pillar of Fore Fife Rail.

In placing them in position, remember that the main topmast stays are set up to lugs which project from the deck in front of the foremast, and the mizzen stay to others in front of the main mast. There must be room for these stays to pass under the fife rails to their attachment points.   It is quite probable that the main fife rail
had side pieces as well as the existing curved rail in front,
and that the sides were removed when the ship was converted to barquentine rig.   To give more places for the
rigging I have made an orthodox fife rail, and so provided
six extra pins on each side (v. Fig. 62).

Deck Lugs for the Stays.—The lugs for the stays must
be made and fixed before the deck is finally fixed in
position.   The shape of them can be seen from the photographs and from Fig. 63.   They should be firmly fixed

to a plate under the deck. They are $\frac{5}{8}$ in. apart, so that the ends of the stays can pass the mast without friction.

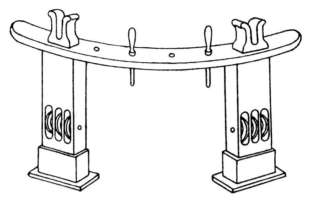

Fig. 60.—Fife Rail on Fore Side of Foremast.

The lugs for the main and mizzen stays are set at a more acute angle than those for the main topmast stay.

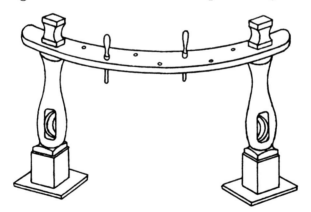

Fig. 61.—Fife Rail on After Side of Foremast. The Pillars are turned and have a single sheave.

In the photograph of the foot of the main mast, the mizzen topmast stay is shown set up to the deck: in Rennie's sail plan it runs to the main-mast top, and I have followed the plan so that only one pair of lugs is needed on the fore side of the main mast.

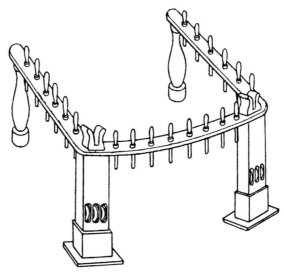

FIG. 62.—The Main Fife Rail, with extra Pins and Side Extensions in the Model. The design of the fore stanchions with their sheaves follows that of the original pillars in the ship.

The Hatchways.—The three hatchways are placed as shown in the diagrams of the deck, and are of the following dimensions :—

Fore   .   .   8 ft. long by 7 ft. 1 in. wide.
Main   .   . 10 ,,   ,,   9 ,, 2 ,, ,,
Aft   .   .   8 ,,   ,,   7 ,, 6 ,, ,,

They are all 18 in. high from the deck to the top of the coaming. The main hatch has a beam or strongback running fore and aft in the centre. Technically, a hatch is one of the solid boards with which the hatchway is covered in. The coaming of the hatchway is the part which stands up from the deck.

In the model the coamings may be built of wood glued and pinned together, or of metal. Around the top edge of the coaming there should be a flat half-round beading, half of which stands up above the edge of the coaming itself. A shelf is thus formed on which the hatches rest. Each hatchway has a slight camber corresponding with the deck camber. At intervals round the sides are projecting right-angled cleats which take the wedges (v. Fig. 64). In order to make a hatchway secure and watertight, tarpaulins are spread over the hatches. The carpenter then comes

FIG. 63.—Deck Lugs for Main and Mizzen Stays. These lugs are firmly bolted under the deck before the deck is finally fixed for keeps. Be sure the opening is large enough to take the stay intended for them, remembering that the main stay is the thickest rope in the ship.

along and turns in the edges of the tarpaulins, and long galvanised-iron hatch bars are placed on the outside of

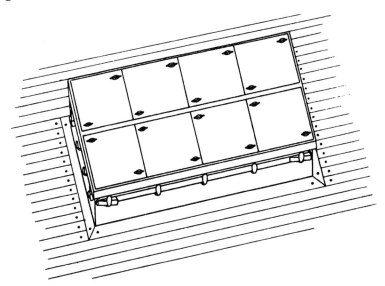

FIG. 64.—The Main Hatch, which is wider than this Sketch makes it appear. Note the wedges driven into the cleats and holding the hatch bar.

turned-in edges. These bars rest in the cleats. Hard-
wood wedges are then driven in between the hatch bar
and the cleats, and the tarpaulin is thus held very securely
clamped against the coaming.

These fittings are very easy to make, and are one of the
details that should not be omitted. The cleats are rather
a monotonous repetition job, about three dozen being
needed. Mine are not the orthodox pattern, which is

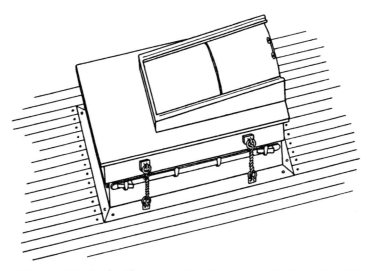

FIG. 65.—The Booby Hatch, lashed to the Deck on the Top of the After-
hatch Coaming.   It has a sliding panel, through which access is
gained to the 'tween decks.

difficult to make. They were made by bending a $\frac{1}{2}$-in.
length of $\frac{1}{16}$-in. wire to a right angle ; one leg was threaded
$\frac{1}{16}$ in., the other leg was flattened out slightly in a vice,
filed square on the inside, and rounded on the outside.
The hatch bars and wooden wedges are very easily made.
All should be black, except the wedges and the hatch bar,
which should be silver plated and then dulled to resemble
galvanised iron. The hatches themselves are of $\frac{1}{16}$-in.
wood, coloured black. Each hatch has two circular

hand-holes at opposite corners, with a wire bar across for lifting.

The Booby Hatch.—The after hatch was used as a companion-way when the ship was carrying emigrants. These were berthed in the 'tween decks, and used the after hatch to come on deck. For convenience, a " booby " hatch was lashed on the top of the after hatch, the lashings passing through the ring-bolts on the deck. The booby hatch was simply a frame a foot high fitting over the permanent hatch (*v.* Fig. 65). It was covered in at the sides, and had a sliding cover in the centre which could be drawn over the companion-way.

There is also a small hatchway 3 ft. 6 in. by 3 ft. 9 in., with a sliding cover, leading down to the crew's quarters, under the main deck in the forecastle. This can only be seen if you look for it under the forecastle deck : it lies immediately aft of the windlass.

The Rail Winches.—Another little fitting which has been mentioned previously but not yet described is the pair of small hand winches which fit under the main rail abaft the main rigging. Each consists of a turned box-wood drum, $\frac{3}{16}$ to $\frac{1}{4}$ in. in diameter, mounted on a spindle with a squared end on which the winch handle fits. A rachet wheel is fixed to the outboard face of the drum, and a pawl suspended above it prevents the drum from rotating backwards. The whole affair is mounted on a vertical metal plate, by means of which it is attached to the main rail (*v.* Fig. 39). These handy rail winches were used to heave on the braces and other gear.

CHAPTER XI.

THE FORECASTLE AND ITS FITTINGS.

Anchors.—Two anchors were always carried on the forecastle head. The old-fashioned wooden stock anchor had not entirely fallen into disuse in the sixties. The *Cutty Sark* has one wooden stock anchor which may or may not be original, and one with a folding iron stock. In the model, for the sake of variety, I have given her two anchors such as she carries at present, and one spare anchor.

Proportions of an Anchor.—An anchor is not such a simple affair as it seems; like everything else about a ship the proportions of its parts are governed by very definite rules. The shank is the central bar of the anchor; it is square in section at the bottom and tapered to two-thirds of its greatest diameter, where it meets the stock. The stock is the wood bar set at right angles to the shank and to the flukes or arms. These are the curved pieces. The length of the flukes from tip to tip measured round the circumference is equal to the length of the shank. The crown is the centre of the flukes; if you stand an anchor on the ground with the ring upwards it will rest upon its crown. The flukes also taper towards their extremities, the point of the fluke being called the bill. The bill is half the size of the fluke in section. To the flukes are attached the palms. The old rule was that the palms should be half the length of the fluke, and should be as broad as they are long. The bill projects slightly beyond the tip of the palm. Just below the stock there should be a shoulder on the shank to keep the stock in its place.

The stock is also made according to definite rules. Its length is equal to that of the shank. It is square in section, and is 1 in. in width for every foot in length. Thus an 8-ft. stock is 8 in. square in section in the middle. Towards the ends it tapers to half its diameter. The top is flat all along its length, and the taper is confined to the sides and bottom of the stock. The central quarter is not affected by the taper. The stock was always made in two halves, and the square hole cut for the shank was made a little bit smaller than the shank, so that when the two halves were clipped on to the shank a small gap remained between them. The halves were held together by iron bands, two or three on each side, which could be knocked up the taper to tighten the hold of the stock on the shank. The shoulder on the shank prevented the stock from slipping down. A hole was formed in the top of the shank through which the ring or shackle was threaded.

A folding stock anchor has the great advantage that it can be stowed easily on deck. The shank has a slightly oval hole where the stock passes through it, to enable the right-angled elbow at one end of the stock to pass through it. Each end of the stock has an acorn-shaped finial. To keep the stock in position when in use there is a flange on the side opposite to the elbow, and a slot cut through it on the other side close up against the shank. Into this slot is driven a wedge-shaped pin, which is loosely chained on to the stock. When the anchor is stowed, the wedge is knocked out, and the stock is pulled up through the hole in the shank so that it can lie parallel with the shank.

Lloyd's Rules Concerning Ground Tackle.—Mr Denny has given me some valuable information regarding the ground tackle required by Lloyd's, and as the ship was built to the rules of, and classed by, Lloyd's, it is quite certain that originally she carried the equipment as laid down in the rules.

In 1868 a sailing ship of the tonnage of the *Cutty Sark* had to carry the following :—

> 3 Bowers, 30 cwts. each, excluding stock.
> 1 Stream, 12 cwts., including stock.
> 2 Kedges, 6 cwts., including stock.
> 2 ,, 3 ,, ,, ,,
> Cables, 1¾ in., 300 fathoms.

The stock weighs 25 per cent. of the bower, so that the full weight of these anchors would be $30 + 7\frac{1}{2}$ cwts.

The third bower was probably carried in the 'tween decks forward, one of the kedges on the poop, or possibly at the break of the poop, and the other kedge and the stream anchor somewhere forward. Very probably they were lashed on the deck abaft the foremast.

Making the Anchors.—The *Cutty Sark's* anchors are 9 ft. 2 in. long from ring to crown, giving a length in the model of $2\frac{1}{4}$ in. Make the shank of $\frac{1}{8}$-in. square brass rod and file it to the proper taper. Silver solder a thick copper-wire ring to the top, and $\frac{1}{4}$ in. below, a thin copper wire to form the shoulder on which the stock rests. Drill a $\frac{3}{64}$-in. hole, and tap it $\frac{1}{16}$ in. in the larger end, for the pin to hold the flukes. For the flukes, take another piece of $\frac{1}{8}$-in. square brass rod $2\frac{1}{4}$ in. long and file the ends to the taper. The edges should be rounded off. Drill a $\frac{1}{16}$-in. hole through the centre. Heat the brass to soften it, and then bend it round a former (*v.* Fig. 66).

The palms can be cut from copper or brass. Two pieces should be sweated together and cut out so that the two palms are of exactly the same shape and size. All the solder must be thoroughly cleaned off before silver soldering the palms on to the flukes : in doing this, remember that the bill projects beyond the palms. The flukes and shank are now joined together by means of a

$\frac{1}{16}$-in. brass screw ; smear some boron compound between the surfaces in contact. Put a fair-sized bit of silver solder in each angle and heat up. Try to get the solder to fill up the angle to a rounded contour. Although the screw is not necessary if you get a good soldered joint, it is worth the extra trouble of putting in, because it holds the parts together in the exact position needed. Without the

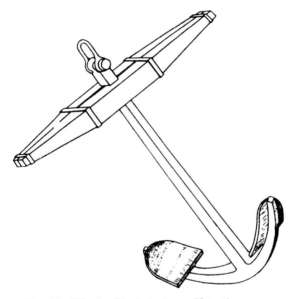

FIG. 66.—Wooden Stock Anchor. Note the gap between the two halves of the stock.

screw the shape of the parts makes this difficult. After cleaning, the end of the screw is filed off and the anchor is ready for its stock. This is made of boxwood to the proportions given and needs no description.

In making the folding stock anchor the shank is made differently, as an expanded portion is needed for the oval hole for the stock. It may either be filed up from the solid or built up by silver soldering the parts together. Personally, I prefer the latter method. The stock is made of wire

about $\frac{3}{32}$ in. in diameter. The acorn-shaped extremities
are turned up on the lathe, drilled, and threaded. The
shoulder and slot are added, and then the wire is bent to
form the elbow. The slot must be drilled on the elbow
side of the stock. I once made the mistake of putting
the shoulder on the elbow side, and of course the anchor
could not be folded up (v. Fig. 67).

Large-sized shackles are fitted to these anchors. When
complete, silver plate and oxidise them : it is a pity
to spoil good metalwork with paint.

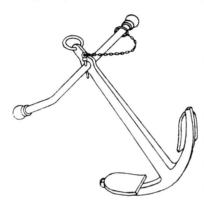

FIG. 67.—Folding Stock Anchor.

The Cables.—The cable
is of the usual studded pattern. It was a general but
not universal custom to unshackle the cables from the
anchors when at sea and
stow them in the chain
locker, so that if the model
is to represent the ship at
sea, the cable need not
appear at all. To the
landsman's eye, however,
absence of the cable might
suggest an appearance of
incompleteness, and a short length of cable should be
made, shackled on to each anchor and led through the
hawse hole.

Anchor chain is always made with studded links.
Each link is 10 in. long, and a chain with five links to the
inch is about the right size. There is a cheap oval-linked
clock chain of this size made of brass stocked by Gray's.
I think I paid 9d. for a 6-ft. length. The parts of the
cable which show should be studded.

It will be found that the gap inside the links is $\frac{1}{16}$ in. :
the studs must be cut to this length, and the ends of each
stud must be filed flat. The quickest way to do this is to

take a scrap of $\frac{1}{16}$-in. plywood; make half a dozen holes
fairly close together in it the size of the wire you are
going to use for the studs. Push the wire through the
holes and nip off the ends so that all the holes are filled;
now file them down flat on one side; press this side on
a bit of steel and file down the other side: you thus get
half a dozen studs of the right size with flat ends, and
enough can be made to do as much of the cable as necessary
in a few minutes.

The studs are fixed with Britinol; a piece of $\frac{1}{8}$-in.
square steel rod is fixed in a small bench vice with about
an inch projecting. Lay the chain on this, link by link;
put a speck of Britinol paste inside each side of the
link, and then put the stud in position. They should be
an easy press fit, otherwise they will move. It will be
found that the Britinol is easier to manage if the link is
just warmed up a little before applying it. If the link is
warm, the paste adheres to it better. A slight whiff with
the blow-pipe will make it run. Any redundant globules
of solder may be detached, and the cable then cleaned
up by rubbing it with a little silver sand between the
palms of the hands. After cleaning, it is silver plated and
oxidised.

Veering Cable.—The great drawback of the old-
fashioned pump up-and-down windlass, to be described
shortly, was that the cable drums could not be disconnected
to allow the cable to run out in the ordinary way. The only
way to get over this difficulty was to pull up the cable and
range it on deck. No sane man drops his anchor without
knowing approximately what the depth of water is, and
a fathom of cable would be ranged on deck for about
every 2 ft. of water, so as to give some scope for veering.
Before the anchor could be let go, it would be necessary
to unshackle the cable at some point conveniently close
to the windlass barrel, take off the one or two turns round
the barrel, and then to shackle the ends of the cable

together again.   It was probably led under the barrel
and not over the top, because a cable running out over the
top of a wooden barrel would very quickly knock it to
bits.

There is a very small hatch, 2 ft. 6 in. square, just in
front of the foremast, which can be clearly seen in the
photograph of the foot of the foremast. This hatch led
down into the chain locker, and on either side of it there
was a chain pipe coming up through the deck.   Although
nothing can be seen of these chain pipes on the deck at
present, they can still be seen in the 'tween decks. Very
often with an arrangement of this sort there was a length
of iron sheathing on the deck between the windlass and
the chain pipes, to protect the deck from being scored
by the cable as it runs out. I do not know whether the
ship's deck was protected in this way, but it is very likely.

Chain Pipes.—Two small chain pipes must be made ;
they go through the deck on each side of the chain locker
hatch, but must be far enough apart for the cable to clear
the sides of the fore hatch.   Each has a solid rounded lip,
which can be soldered on. If the cable is shown ranged on
deck it will go down through these pipes, but if the cable
is not shown, the openings of the pipes are plugged with
a solid oak stopper to prevent the water from running
down them.

The chain locker hatch can be made of a solid block,
as it is only ¼ in. high ; it lies between the lugs for the
main-topmast stay.

Anchor Release Gear.—There were several ingenious
mechanical contrivances in use in sailing ships for releasing
the anchor. The mechanism in the *Cutty Sark* is attached
to the front side of the cathead, and consists of two main
parts (*v.* Fig. 68). There is a stout pin about 6 in. long
outside the bulwarks, pivoted to the cathead at its outer
end. The inner end of this pin rests in a grooved support,
which is attached to a stout shaft passing through the

bulwarks. The inboard end of this shaft has a curved hand-lever welded to its end. On pulling the lever forward, the shaft is rotated about $\frac{3}{8}$ths of a circle. The grooved support also rotates, so that the groove on its upper surface now faces downwards and forwards, with the result that the pin drops out. When the ship was nearing land, the anchors were swung outboard and the pin of the release gear was threaded through the shackle, so that the anchor

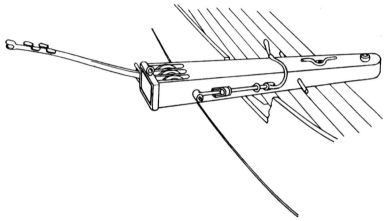

Fig. 68.—The Port Cathead and Whisker. The anchor release gear is shown in front of the cathead with the forecastle bulwark cut away. The anchor shackle was threaded on to the pivoted pin outside, which fell down on pulling the lever forward and so released the anchor.

was suspended beneath the cathead by the pin and could be let go immediately by simply pulling on the lever of the gear.

This gear is very simple to make, and should certainly be included in the fittings of the ship.

Getting the Anchor Inboard.—Anchor davits were only fitted to the later big steel carriers, but one never sees them in any pictures or photographs of the earlier wooden or composite ships. The anchors had to be got on deck by hand, and as a 9-ft. anchor would weigh nearly a couple of tons, it must have been a somewhat strenuous exercise. It was first raised by the three-fold purchase in the cathead. A short wire strop with an eye at each end was then passed round the shank close to the flukes. Another three-fold purchase block with a large hook, called the fish hook, was then hooked into the eyes of this strop. The other end of the purchase was attached to a long wire pendant, which was put over the topmast head. This pendant was not a fixture, but was only rigged for the purpose of fishing the anchor. It was a long wire rope with a spliced eye at each end. The top end was taken round the topmast head and shackled to its own part; the upper block of the purchase shackled to the lower eye. By hoisting on this purchase the anchor could be lifted, and with some manipulation deposited in its proper place on the forecastle deck.

Catheads.—These are two stout pieces of timber which project outboard from the forecastle head (*v.* Fig. 26). They are 9 ft. in length, 3 ft. of which is outside the bulwarks. The outside portion is square in section and measures 14 in. across. The lower surface of the inboard 6 ft. is tapered so that when this surface is resting on the deck the whole of the cathead has an upward slant. This inboard portion was firmly bolted to the deck beams underneath. It has a large cleat on the top and a stout iron bar through it in a fore and aft direction. The anchor release gear is attached to its front surface.

The outboard end is slotted for the three sheaves which form part of the gear for catting the anchor. An iron band encircles the extreme end of the cathead; on the top of this band is welded an important iron ring, which gives attachment to the fore tack when the yards are braced up. To the after side of the band is welded a bracket in which the whisker rests. The outward facing end of cathead was generally ornamented with a cat's face carved in relief; some builders, such as Hall's of Aberdeen, used this position to put their trade-mark on a ship.

The catheads are best made out of boxwood, and the iron band, etc., built up of copper, and oxidised in the way previously described. They are painted black.

The Whiskers.—From the after side of each cathead projects a stout iron bar called the whisker. Its inner extremity is pivoted to the cathead close to the bulwarks ; 3 ft. out it rests in the above-mentioned bracket. This part of the whisker is square in section. Beyond the cathead it becomes round in section and is bent back at an obtuse angle. The function of the whisker is to spread out the jibboom guys. There are three of these, and three cleats are forged on the whisker to take them. The outermost one is at the extreme end and the other two are on the top of the whisker about a foot apart. A light pin passes through each cleat to prevent the guys from jerking out. The whiskers are pivoted, so that when the ship is alongside a wharf they can be folded up and be got out of the way. They are painted white.

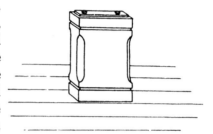

FIG. 69.—Towing Post or Mooring Post on Forecastle Head. The posts are stepped on the main deck and may originally have formed part of the old windlass.

Towing Posts.—On the forecastle deck there are two large towing posts 18 in. high, oblong in section, 15 in. by 6 in. These pass down through the deck, and are bedded in the main deck just abaft the windlass. Mr Denny suggests that these posts were part of the original windlass (*v.* Fig. 69).

Most people who are interested in the *Cutty Sark* have read Lubbock's book. Although it does not set out to give any minute description of the ship, one can pick up from it here and there little scraps of internal evidence about her arrangements.

On p. 313 there is a description of a rough passage from China to Sydney. The watch was on the forecastle head, heaving down the fore tack with the capstan, when a green sea came over and washed them all off, except the third mate, who " got caught up on one of the arms of the windlass."

Evidently, therefore, in addition to the capstan there was a windlass, and it had arms. The only sort of windlass with arms which was in use in those days was known, I believe, as the Armstrong patent. So I have given my model a capstan and a windlass of this pattern. The windlass was used only for weighing the anchor.

The Capstan.—The present capstan is a cast-iron one of the usual pattern, with a double head. It has two rows of square holes for the capstan bars, one above the other. By working the capstan through the upper holes gears are actuated which give increased power. The shaft of the capstan passes through the deck and terminates in a bevel gear which drives the windlass. This is of the ordinary pattern, with chain drum brakes, etc., for veering and taking in the cable. All this gear was placed on board while under Portuguese ownership.

It is probable that originally there was a capstan on the forecastle head which was used not for getting in the cable but for catting the anchor, and for heaving down the fore tack. The windlass was driven by two long levers athwartships with cross-bars at the outer end. The men pumped these levers up and down. They were inserted into a rocker centrally pivoted to a samson post. Connecting links ran from each end of the rocker through the deck to a dog, which engaged the teeth of a gear wheel. These gears were firmly bolted on to the wooden barrel of the winch, and the up-and-down pumping motion thus became a rotary motion by which the cable was slowly but surely taken in. This somewhat primitive type of windlass is still used on the lighters and barges frequenting the port of Hull. The great drawback of it is that the cable cannot be veered by simply easing off the brake.

The Windlass.—Making up a windlass of this pattern

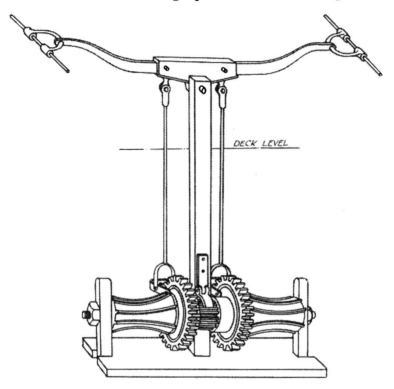

FIG. 70.—The Old " Jig-y-Jig " Windlass. This drawing was made from the model of the windlass housed beneath the forecastle deck, where it is very difficult to see it. The arms could be unshipped and stowed away.

proved quite an interesting bit of work. The visible part of it above the deck is a simple soldering job and needs no description. The photograph of the forecastle head shows it well, and also the drawing (*v.* Fig. 70) made from the actual model windlass. To construct it, I obtained two solid brass gear wheels $\frac{5}{8}$ in. in diameter, about $\frac{3}{32}$ in.

wide, and turned a square groove on each face close to the
circumference. The mechanism for turning the gears can
be understood from the small sketch more easily than
from a description (*v.* Fig. 71). Each gear has on its forward side two arms connected by a cross-bar in front.
The after end of each arm has a stud which works in
the groove cut in the gear. A dog is pivoted between the
arms, and the pin on which it is pivoted also carries the
ends of the fork, to the top of which the lever coming

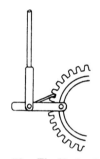

through the deck is screwed. When
the lever is pushed down the arms
are pushed down, and slide circum-
ferentially round the gear owing to
the action of the studs in the groove.
The dog clicks over the teeth. When
the lever is pulled up the dog catches
in the teeth and turns the gear round,
so that the action is a very simple
one. While the windlass is being
worked, one of the levers is always
pulling upwards, and therefore there
is a continuous rotation.

Fig. 71.—The Mechanism
actuating the Wind-
lass Gears. The stud
slips round in the
groove cut on the side
of the gear wheel.

The samson post stands between
the two gear wheels ; on the axle there
is a third gear, much smaller, which lies between and is
solidly connected with the two large ones. A wide pawl is
hinged to the samson post, and by meshing with this third
gear prevents the windlass from turning backwards.

Outside the large gears are the barrels of the windlass,
also bolted to the gears, so that everything on the axle,
the three gears and the two barrels, turn together. The
bearings are housed in two solid posts with strong knees
on the forward side.

This windlass is under the forecastle head of the model,
and can only just be seen by bending down. I left it silver
plated and not oxidised, so that it can be seen with a little

less difficulty. It is fixed on the forward side of the hatch leading to the old quarters of the crew.

Making the Capstan.—The capstan is made from a piece of hexagon brass rod $\frac{1}{2}$ in. across the flats. Drill a $\frac{1}{16}$-in. hole at the centre of each flat, and square these by tapping in a little toothed drift, which can easily be made out of a scrap of silver steel and hardened. A square needle file can also be used if the holes are drilled right through. The capstan is then turned up to shape in the lathe (v. Fig. 72). Before parting off from the rod the flutes are cut in the barrel. File up a circular cutter from a piece of $\frac{3}{8}$-in. silver steel to the shape of the flutes. The cutter is mounted in the chuck and the capstan held by its hexagon stalk in the tool rest. A flute can then be cut for each hexagon face. Part off, face up the bottom, centre drill $\frac{7}{64}$ in. and tap $\frac{1}{8}$ in. for the central pivot. Four or more pawls are attached to the lower part of the

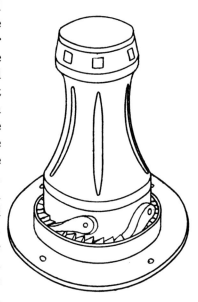

FIG. 72.—The Capstan on the Model has a Single Head. The geared capstan on the ship at present is not original. The old capstan was not used for getting the anchor, but only for catting it and heaving on various purchases.

capstan, and a toothed ring is filed out—if you have no gear-cutting tools—to fit the bottom of the capstan. This toothed ring is set inside another ring turned to an angle section. Plate and oxidise it.

Capstan Bars.—The capstan bars, six in number, are $1\frac{3}{4}$ in. long. They are square sectioned at one end, rounded, and slightly tapered at the other. Make them of boxwood, and also two pairs of little racks which fit on the after side of the lavatories.

Other Details on Forecastle Head.—On the forecastle head there is a large ring-bolt midway between the capstan and the samson post of the windlass. In the after corners behind the anchors are bollards and two more ring-bolts.

Forward of the cathead there is a plate $\frac{1}{8}$ in. by $\frac{5}{8}$ in. long with three ring-bolts for the jibsheets. The fore-topmast stay sailsheet was hooked to the ring-bolt close to the bollards.

The deck planking of the forecastle head is peculiar, in that the central portion of the planking is wider than that at the sides, being 9 in. instead of 6 in. The planking is joggled along its whole length into a joggling plank fixed inside the margin plank, which is a continuation of the main rail forward.

The bulwarks are only 15 in. high, and are surmounted by the top rail ; this rail is 9 in. wide, but tapers off as it runs aft to 6 in. at the break of the forecastle head. Two-ball stanchions 2 ft. 6 in. high are mounted on this rail. There are seven on each side, or eight if one includes the short stanchion mounted on the knighthead. There are screwed sleeves on the rail, part of which can be detached in order to get the anchors over the side.

Stanchions.—Altogether about four dozen stanchions are needed ; they can be built up of brass wire and silver balls. These hollow balls are obtainable from Gray's in very small sizes, and each has a small hole ; this hole must be enlarged to take the wire, and drilled through the opposite pole so that the wire can be threaded through. Britinol paste is pushed into the ball before it is threaded, and then the wire is heated gently with the blow-pipe. Some of the solder bubbles out, but is sucked back again on cooling. Any excess of solder is taken off with a running-down cutter. The upper ball is prepared by enlarging the hole in it. The wire is cut off $\frac{5}{16}$ in. above the ball with the aid of a simple little jig. The upper ball is then soldered on to the wire.

Both balls are now drilled transversely, together with the wire inside them, and the holes must correspond in direction. A perfectly simple way of doing this without a jig, which should be of steel and rather difficult to make, is as follows :—

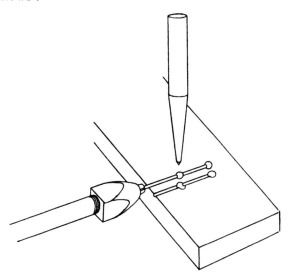

FIG. 73.—This Diagram clarifies the explanation of the Method described for Drilling Stanchion Balls. Both sides of the balls are dotted, and the square faces of the square nut act as guides.

Make a couple of indentations in a flat piece of wood to take the balls ; hold the end of the wire in a pin vice with a square nut (*v.* Fig. 73). Lay the pin vice on the bench with one face of the nut flat and the balls in their indentations. With a fine centre-punch dot the top of the balls. Turn the pin vice over so that the face of the nut which was flat on the bench is now uppermost, and dot the balls again. Drill from both sides at the dots and the holes will come right. I think the best drills to use are watchmakers' No. 8, and I find that dipping the point in oil helps a lot. Sometimes, if there is not enough solder inside the ball the drill will tend to slip off the wire inside the ball instead of going through it. The bases of the stanchions are most easily made by parting off thin slices of a suitable bouchon wire ; this material is most useful for several purposes, as it saves one the trouble of centring

FIG. 74.—The Forecastle Head of the Model. The capstan bars are in racks on the after side of the heads. The Samson post and working handles of the windlass lie between the anchors, aft of the capstan.

and drilling small rod. The stanchions are painted white, and any solder stains are thus covered up. The poop stanchions are also two-ball and of the same height. The monkey poop stanchions have only one ball at the top.

The Heads.—The heads, the name given to the men's lavatories at the break of the forecastle, are built up on the blocks which support the after edge of the forecastle deck. An upper block of wood is cut out to the shape of the upper half of the head and dowelled to fit on to the lower half, which is already fixed (v. Figs. 5 and 74). The door and its framework, the fore and after sides, and the curved roof, all made of $\frac{1}{32}$-in. 3-ply, are glued and pinned to the upper half, which when painted white is fixed to the lower half. The door frame and the after side are made deep enough to lie below the level of the teak deck. The outer edge of the after side is cut at an angle to fit into the bulwark, which is flared outwards at this point. Owing to the curvature of the roof it is unsafe to trust to glue alone, and it must therefore be securely pinned on to the solid block underlying it.

The pigsty is on the port side, under the forecastle, immediately on the fore side of the head. Owing to the shape of the supporting block it cannot be made of the full and proper depth athwartships. However, by painting the inner surface of the supporting block black the effect of depth is obtained. All that need be made is a framework of wood holding a row of vertical wire rods. The whole of this is painted white and glued in position.

The paint locker on the starboard side is made up by glueing strips of $\frac{1}{32}$ in. half-round boxwood in the form of squares on to a suitably shaped piece of 3-ply. This gives the effect of several cupboards. It is also painted white.

CHAPTER XII.

THE POOP AND ITS FITTINGS.

The Poop.—Behind the mizzen mast the deck is raised
4 ft. This part would be called the quarter deck in a
naval ship, and was known as the poop in the merchant
service. It is mainly occupied by a raised coach-house
top or monkey poop over the cabin accommodation (*v.*
Fig. 75).

The Poop Deck.—The deck of the poop is planked in
the ordinary way. Between the coach-house top and the
break of the poop there is a narrow passage, 2 ft. 9 in.
wide, leading to the doors of the companion. The planking here runs athwartships. Some of the planks round the
stern require joggling into the margin plank, but as the
planking approaches the middle line they are not joggled.
The shipwright rule about this has been previously mentioned. The margin plank round the stern is difficult to
make nicely. The radius of the curve is too small to allow
of bending the teak, and it must therefore be cut out in
one or more pieces. There is a mitred surround to the
coach-house roof.

The Monkey Poop.—The dimensions of the coach-house
top are 31 ft. long, 16 ft. 9 in. wide at the after end,
21 ft. 3 in. at the fore end. The height is 2 ft. 6 in. There
is a slight camber on the roof; the side walls are not
quite straight in line, but curve slightly to correspond
with the run of the ship. There are five port holes in each
side, two on the aft, and two on the forward wall. Between

Fig. 75.—This magnificent Photograph, taken from the Fore Rigging, is of great personal interest. Captain Woodget, twenty-seven years after leaving the ship, is again at the wheel, and Captain Millett, who served part of his apprenticeship in the ship, is standing beside him. Apart from its historical interest the photograph is very rich in details of the rigging, and shows the plan of the poop.

(*By courtesy of the "Daily Mirror."*)

the port holes oblongs of panelling relieve the flatness.
The part can be built up of strips of wood $\frac{11}{16}$ in. wide, the
fore and aft walls having raised pieces added to them to
fit the camber of the roof, which should be about $\frac{1}{8}$ in.
They are glued and pinned together with shaped blocks
in the corners to make it secure. The port holes are drilled
$\frac{7}{32}$ in., and the panelling is put on. This may most conveniently be made up as described in the section on the
deck houses, the moulding being a simple half-round
drawn from $\frac{1}{32}$-in. boxwood stringing.

Fourteen port holes are required. The method of
making them has been already described.

The roof of the coach-house top is planked with strips
of teak $\frac{1}{32}$ in. thick. Make the under deck of $\frac{1}{16}$-in. 3-ply,
and screw this on to two $\frac{1}{2}$-in. by $\frac{1}{4}$-in. shaped battens to
keep the camber. The ends of these battens must press
against the side walls to give the latter the slight outward
curvature. They are, of course, arranged so that they do
not abut against the port holes.

The Skylight.—A large skylight gives light and air to
the saloon. It is 9 ft. 6 in. long, and has three lights on
each side, each being 3 ft. square. There is a bar between
the lights : the bars are $\frac{3}{32}$ in. wide and the lights $\frac{3}{4}$ in.
This allows of a very slight overlap of the lights at each
end. The frame is built up of thin strip wood, and the
top bar $\frac{1}{4}$ in. wide between the lights makes it rigid. The
lights are made of $\frac{3}{32}$-in. by $\frac{1}{32}$-in. strip mitred at the
joints, with a central bar. To ensure making them to same
size a jig should be used. They are glued on to strips of
paper, which can be cut away when the glue is firmly
set. The glass may be real glass. In microscopical work
very thin " cover glasses " are used, a common size being
$\frac{3}{4}$ in. If these are used, they are best fixed to the wood
with Canada balsam, otherwise celluloid can be substituted for glass. Each light has two hinges. These are
squeezed round a thin wire in a vice from a strip of shim

brass $\frac{3}{1000}$ in. thick and $\frac{3}{32}$ in. wide. Fine slots are cut for them in the top bar, and they can be slipped in after the lights have been fixed in position and the painting of the skylight is complete. It is white in colour.

The Companion.—During the Portuguese ownership a companion was cut in the after wall of the coach-house top on the starboard side. The original companion is still in existence, and is situated centrally immediately behind the mizzen mast. It has a door on either side leading on to the narrow gangway of the coach-house top. This part of the companion is 3 ft. 9 in. wide and 6 ft. 6 in. high. It extends aft for 4 ft. 6 in. The roof is flat in front, and as it runs aft it curves downwards over the extension to meet the coach-house roof. The roof is white, and the rest of the companion is polished teak or mahogany.

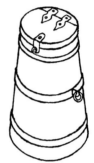

Harness Casks.—Lashed to ring-bolts in the roof between the skylight and the companion are two " harness casks." I do not know how they got this name. One contained salt beef and the other salt pork. They are conical in shape, the base being $\frac{5}{8}$ in. and the height $\frac{3}{4}$ in.

FIG. 76.—One of the Harness Casks. They stand on battens on the poop-house roof abaft the companion.

There are three brass bands round each (*v.* Fig. 76). They can be turned up from some close-grained wood, stained, and varnished. The lids are separately turned and put on after the bands are fixed. The lids are divided with the hinges on the top and a hasp in front so that they can be padlocked. They should really be oval in section, but are difficult to make.

Binnacle.—In front of the wheel there is a binnacle fixed to the roof. The helmsman always stood on the weather of the wheel, and the binnacle would not be directly in front of him. It is a little brass turning $\frac{3}{8}$ in.

in height. Two pointed bits of wire are soldered to the sides to represent the lamps. (*v.* Fig. 77).

Bell.—The bell is hung in a frame within reach of the helmsman (*v.* Fig. 78). It can be turned up from $\frac{5}{16}$-in. brass rod. There is also a bell in the fore part of the ship. It can be slung either from the mainstay just in front of the fore-deck house or from the forestay, so as to be within reach of the lookout on the forecastle head. I have not been able to ascertain definitely where it was originally.

FIG. 77.
The Binnacle.

FIG. 78.—The Old Bell of the Ship, fixed on the After Edge of the Monkey Poop in front of the Wheel.

Along each side of the coach-house roof there is a railing 3-ft. high in single-ball stanchions. The rail itself curves down to the roof fore and aft. There are six stanchions on each side.

There is a small open coal stove in the saloon against the fore bulkhead on the port side, and a small metal chimney $\frac{1}{8}$ in. in diameter is led up from it through the roof; a piece of copper tube $1\frac{1}{2}$ in. high with a cowl at the top and a flange at the bottom, oxidised black, represents this.

The port-side after corner is occupied by a W.C., which discharges through an opening in the counter. There is a mushroom ventilator over it in the roof.

The Bucket Rail.—The gangway leading to the companion is protected by a heavy teak rail supported on three turned pillars aside. The rail is $\frac{1}{4}$ in. wide, $\frac{1}{16}$ in.

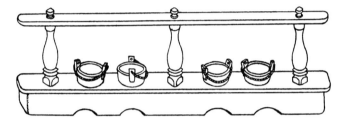

FIG. 79.—Bucket Rail with Four Buckets at Break of the Poop.

thick, and $2\frac{3}{8}$ in. long. The turned pillars pass through the rail and terminate in small acorn-shaped finials. The pillars themselves are $\frac{9}{16}$ in. high, squared at their base. These small pillars and others like them are most easily turned out of bone knitting needles. To square the base, leave a stalk on the turning and hold it by this in a pin vice with a square nut; the faces of the nut act as guides for filing the base square. The pillars are painted white. They are fitted into a rack which holds four fire-buckets on each side. These racks are finished bright, and may be made of thin mahogany $\frac{5}{16}$ in. wide. The space between the pillars is $\frac{7}{8}$ in., and this is occupied by two $\frac{1}{4}$-in. holes spaced $\frac{1}{8}$ in. from the pillars and from each other (v. Fig. 79). The best way to drill comparatively large holes in thin

veneer is to clamp it between two strips of thicker stuff
and drill through the three. The veneer will not then be
torn or split. The bucket racks rest on uprights $\frac{3}{16}$ in.
high; the bottom edges of these are not straight, but
have segments of circles cut out of them so that water
may run underneath. They are set $\frac{1}{16}$ in. behind the fore
edge of the poop deck. This fore edge is of teak moulded
to a half-round, and overhangs the main deck $\frac{1}{8}$ in. A
brass hand-rail for the poop ladders is attached to the
outer ends of the teak rail.

The Buckets.—I tried various ways of making the
buckets, and found the simplest and easiest was to turn
them out of boxwood. A tool was made to hollow out the
inside. This was a piece of $\frac{1}{4}$-in. round silver steel, turned
to a cone of correct size; half the cone was filed away and
a cutting edge formed on the edges. A cutting edge was
also filed on the narrow end of the cone. A piece of round
boxwood was centred and bored to a depth of $\frac{1}{4}$ in. with a
$\frac{3}{16}$-in **D**-bit. The conical tool then finished the boring.
The outside was then shaped with a sharp, flat spring-tool
set at the appropriate angle; the sides should be $\frac{1}{32}$-in.
thick; the bucket is then parted off. The diameter of
the bottom of the buckets is $\frac{7}{32}$ in. and the top $\frac{9}{32}$ in.; the
height is $\frac{5}{16}$ in. Each bucket was then fitted with a pair
of ears drilled $\frac{1}{32}$ in. to take the rope handle, which is
made of white surgical silk. The inside is painted white
and the outside stained and polished. In making these
buckets, it may be noted that they should be bored before
being turned on the outside; if they are turned first, the
boring tool may easily split the thin sides.

Pin Rail.—Under the mizzen rigging there is a small
rail with five belaying pins $1\frac{1}{4}$ in. long, $\frac{3}{16}$ in. wide, $\frac{11}{16}$ in.
high, supported on two turned legs painted white. As
there is only a spider band round the mizzen, with eight
pins and no fife rail at its foot, obviously more places are
required for turning up the mizzen rigging together with

the main topgallant, royal and skysail braces, not to mention the spanker gear. It is, therefore, reasonable to suppose that this small pin rail was at some time substituted for a much larger one, and I have made them to run from the topmast backstays aft for 2 in., and given them ten pins aside.

Other fittings on the poop are a pair of bollards on each side, abaft the rigging; these are $\frac{1}{4}$ in. high, $\frac{3}{16}$ in. across top, and $\frac{5}{8}$ in. long on the base. Ring-bolts for the halliards are screwed into the covering board under the rigging, and a pair farther aft for the range. Opposite the end of the emergency tiller there is another pair of large ring-bolts attached to a large U-shaped deck plate. These ring-bolts could be used either for the spanker boom-sheets or for a block, if ever it were necessary to rig the emergency steering tackle.

The Wheel.—This is a most intriguing fitting to make, and presents no particular difficulty. The rim is first turned up of boxwood, and should be divided and drilled for the eight spokes before being parted off. If your lathe has no division plate, the division must be done with the help of one of the screw-cutting gear wheels which has a number of teeth divisible by eight. The hub is made of brass. Chuck a stout length of $\frac{1}{4}$-in. screw rod, face, centre, drill $\frac{7}{64}$ in., and tap $\frac{1}{8}$ in. Turn down a spigot $\frac{1}{16}$ in. $\frac{5}{32}$ in. in diameter; then turn out a square-sectioned groove $\frac{1}{16}$ in. wide and deep. Part off $\frac{1}{16}$ in. beyond this. Screw a short-length $\frac{1}{8}$-in. rod into the tapped hole, and holding it by this in the chuck, turn up the reverse face to a rounded boss. The spokes are then turned out of a bone knitting needle and their inner ends filed square $\frac{1}{16}$ in. bare, with the aid of a pin vice, as previously described. A fine hole is drilled in the outer end of each spoke, into which a wire is pushed through the corresponding hole in the rim and so fixes it to the rim. The square ends of the spokes are fixed in the square groove in the boss with

Ashe's dental cement. The projecting ends of the spokes by which the wheel is gripped are also turned from bone, each being $\frac{1}{8}$ in. long, with a little spigot to fix it in the rim ; one of these is larger than the others :, this spoke should be at the top of the wheel when the rudder is in a central position. The spigots can also be fixed in the rim with dental cement. The boss of the wheel is polished brass, the rim and spokes are stained brown, and the projecting ends of the spokes may be left in the natural bone colour. The boss is 2 ft. 6 in. from the edge of the coach-house roof. The steering gear is contained in an oblong-shaped box behind the wheel. The lid of this box is in two halves and hinged, so that either side can be lifted up to allow the gear to be inspected and kept properly oiled. It is supported on four short turned legs ; the two forward legs are a little longer than the two aft, because the axis of the steering-gear box is not parallel with the deck, but at right angles with the rudder stock. The box is $1\frac{3}{4}$ in. long, $\frac{3}{4}$ in. wide ; the two halves of the lid are $\frac{7}{16}$ in. wide, and the forward pair of legs $\frac{3}{8}$ in. long. The sides of the box have a long oval panel on which the ship's name was carved, often in a scroll of decorative work. The name was embossed, and printed in gold on white paper and cut out to fit the panel. On lifting the lid of the box the actual steering-gear is seen. This consists of a long, square threaded screw which is turned by the steering-wheel. One half of this screw is right-hand and the other half left-hand threaded, the latter being on the forward side. Upon each portion of the screw is mounted a large rounded nut. On the outer side of each nut is a projecting lug, through which a hole is bored horizontally. Through this hole a guide rod passes which is fixed fore and aft in the metal framework of the steering-gear. The object of this rod is to prevent the nut turning over when the screw is rotated. It must, therefore, move either forward or backward according to the direction of the rotation of the wheel. Jointed to the under side of each lug by a pin is a lever. The lever attached to the after nut is long, that to the forward nut is short. The forward ends of these levers are jointed by pins to the transverse bar on the rudder head which constitutes the tiller. The action of the gear is quite simple, the main mechanical feature being that the two nuts will always either approach or recede from each other on turning the wheel, owing to one being on a right-hand and the other on a left-hand thread. The levers transmit this motion to the tiller, and in this way the rudder is moved. The mechanism must be arranged so that when the wheel is turned to port, the rudder, and therefore the ship's head, are turned to port also, and vice versa. It will depend upon whether the right or the left hand part of the thread is in front and connecting up the levers to the tiller accordingly.

In order to familiarise myself with the mechanical details of the gear I made it up, using $\frac{1}{8}$-in. ordinary Whitworth thread, for which one can obtain a left-hand tap and die. The wheel will therefore move rudder to port or starboard. This, however, is somewhat a work of supererogation, as the whole affair is hidden by the lid of the box. The details of the mechanism, however, will interest those who want to know how things work in a ship (v. Fig. 80).

In addition to the transverse tiller a fore and aft tiller is fixed to the rudder head, projecting backwards under the box about 6 in. above the deck. Two eyes are welded on to the after end, into which the emergency tackles can be hooked in the event of the main steering-gear breaking down—an accident which was not entirely unknown.

Square Gratings.—A square grating was laid on either side of the steering-wheel for the helmsman to stand upon (v. Fig. 81), so obviating constant wear on one spot of the deck, not, as one might have supposed, to keep his

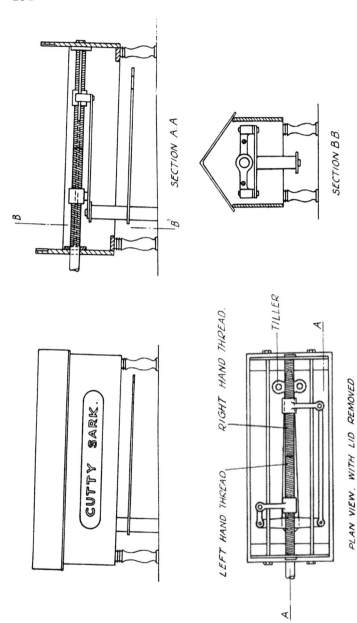

SECTION A.A

SECTION B B.

PLAN VIEW. WITH LID REMOVED.

RIGHT HAND THREAD.

LEFT HAND THREAD

TILLER

CUTTY SARK.

FIG. 80.—The Steering-gear Box and Mechanism.   The gear is set at right angles with the rudder stock, not with the deck.   The emergency tiller runs aft under the box.   The mechanical details of the gear can be readily grasped from this drawing, which was made from the actual gear in the model.

feet dry. These square gratings are rather a bugbear, and are most horrible and finicky things to make. One can get some sort of result by drilling holes in thin wood and squaring them with a drift and file, but it is very difficult to keep the holes in line. In full-sized work these gratings are made by halved joints in 1½ in. square stuff, and the holes are 1½ in. square. I made them of boxwood stringing, slightly over $\frac{1}{32}$ in. square. The first difficulty is to get such small stuff really square. It looks square, but is not, when one buys it. To square it, take a piece of tin-plate with a straight-edge. In this edge file a very small square slot. If you can do this the first difficulty is defeated. All that is needed is to draw the stringing through the square, holding the piece of tin down on a flat metal surface. It takes about a yard of stringing to make a grating about 1 in. square. Having squared the boxwood, prepare and square to the same size some softer and darker coloured wood, such as satin walnut.

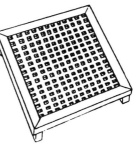

Fig. 81.—A Squared Grating —also a cure for impatience.

First, cut as many strips 1 in. long as, placed alongside each other, will make them altogether as nearly as possible 1 in. wide. The ends of these 1-in. strips should be square. Now make a mitred surround in boxwood strip $\frac{3}{32}$ in. and about $\frac{1}{32}$ in. thick. Glue this on to a piece of squared drawing-paper, leaving out the side member on the right hand. The 1-in. long strips should pack closely into the surround. Leave the glue to set firmly before proceeding, and in the meantime cut some dozens of pieces about ⅛ in. long, of which one end at least should be square. I will call these pegs. A great aid to one's eyes in doing this sort of fine work is to do the cutting on a flat piece of black vulcanite.

When the surround is firmly set, pack in the 1-in. strips. I should have mentioned that they should be an odd number, and the size of the surround and grating must be arranged to accommodate an odd number. The reason for this is that half the strips only act as guides and are withdrawn, and that the first and last strip abutting against the top and bottom members of the surround are among those withdrawn. Withdraw the top and every other one, including the bottom one, about a third of their length sideways through the open right-hand side of the surround.

Now withdraw the even members about $\frac{1}{8}$ in. and paint the paper and inner edge of the left-hand member of the surround with glue. I find Page's liquid cold glue suitable for the work. Push back the even members so that they are caught in the glue. and butt cleanly up against the left-hand surround member. Your eye will tell you if the spacing is even. If not, the odd members must be pushed up again a little, but not into the glue, to get the spacing right. The next step is to glue a strip of the satin walnut, which has been drawn to the same size as the boxwood strip, at right angles to the boxwood strips. Its left-hand edge must exactly correspond with the right-hand edge of the left-hand member of the surround. In effect it covers the first row of square holes. Now, with a fine pair of forceps pick up one of the pegs and put it with its square end downwards into the gap between the top member of the surround and the second 1-in. strip, pressing it close up against the satin walnut strip. Before putting it into position drop in a tiny drop of glue. Put in the pegs down the line against the satin walnut, and when they are all in position paint them freely with glue. It is at once apparent when one begins to put in the pegs how important it is that they should be really square, otherwise they would not properly fit the gaps. Having got in a row of pegs, glue on a second piece of satin walnut, pressing it firmly up against the pegs. This has the effect of squeezing them up into a straight line. The lines on the squared paper will help you to keep the lines fair and square. Continue to put in a row of pegs and a satin walnut strip alternately until the surround is filled up, or you have got tired of the job, the guide or spacing strips being gradually withdrawn. If the end row should come as pegs, a little must be cut off the ends of the surrounds, because a row of holes must come next to the surround. The right-hand member of the surround can then be put in. The soaking with glue may tend to make the paper, which should be as thin as possible, buckle a little. If so, put a weight on the top and leave the grating to settle for a couple of days.

The next proceeding when the glue is thoroughly set is to saw through the tops of the last row of pegs at the level of the surround. I use for this a fine jeweller's hack-saw blade, which is the finest thing in saws I possess. Then the satin walnut is removed, and afterwards the tops of the second row of pegs, and so on, until the whole grating is clear.

It should now be rubbed on fine glass-paper. Avoid rubbing in the direction of the 1-in. strips ; this tends to dislodge the minute ends of the pegs. Rub across the 1-in. strips and the parts will keep in place. The paper underneath is also removed by rubbing the grating on glass-paper. Blow out the dust, and with a fine square file touch up the corners, which have been filled with glue to restore the sharp outline of the square holes.

The whole process is tedious and somewhat trying to the eyes, but I have not been able to improve upon it, and the result is, although not perfect, very near the real thing. A more skilful enthusiast might saw evenly spaced slots to an even depth through the 1-in. strips placed side by side, and so halve the joints and make a splendid job of it.

The Log.—The poop requires one more interesting little fitting, and that is the log-line and log-ship (*v.* Fig. 82). They were usually kept attached to the rail on the port quarter. This apparatus was used to ascertain the speed of the ship before patent logs came into use.

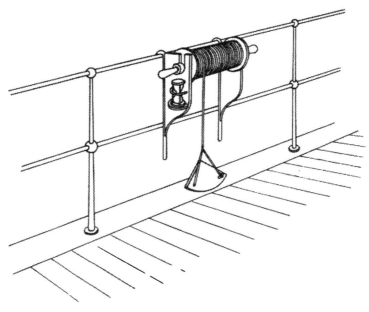

Fig. 82.—The old-fashioned and, let it be whispered, inaccurate, Log-line and Log-ship, suspended on the Poop Rail. Note the sand-glass and one end of the line fastened to the log-ship by a wooden peg. The deck planking in this drawing should be running fore and aft.

The log-ship was a piece of wood about 2 ft. wide, shaped like the sector of a circle; the arc was weighted by a strip of lead let into its edge, so that it would float upright in the water. There were two holes, one at each end of the arc; a piece of line about 8 ft. long was threaded through one of these holes and knotted behind, and the other end was fitted to a wooden peg which was a good fit, but not too tight, in the other hole. To the centre of this piece of line was attached the log-line proper, which was kept coiled on a drum with a handle at each end, made so that the drum could revolve freely on the handles. The log-line was marked at intervals with knots and bits of leather and bunting. The third essential part of the apparatus was a sand-glass.

Two men or boys were required to heave the log. It was always thrown overboard on the lee quarter. One boy held the log-line drum by the handles above his head ; the other boy then pulls off several fathoms of the line and drops the log-ship over the side. As there is plenty of stray line with it in the water, it will not be pulled along behind the ship but will remain at a fixed point in the water, and as the ship goes forward from it the line will begin to run off the drum. The first boy now concentrates his attention on the sand-glass, while the boy holding the drum watches the line as it runs out. At a certain point a piece of white bunting is tied to the line, and directly this touches the rail the boy calls out " turn," which is the signal for turning over the sand-glass. As soon as the glass runs out the first boy calls out " stop," and the second boy catches hold of the line and stops it from running out any more. The result of this is that the ship is now towing the log-ship, and the pressure of the water against it is so great that the wooden peg is pulled out, and it can then be easily hauled aboard along the surface of the water.

There are marks at frequent intervals on the line, so that the length of line between the piece of white bunting and the point where the second boy stopped it can easily be ascertained. That will be the distance the ship has travelled in the space of time it has taken the sand-glass to run out. The timing of the sand-glass and the marking of the log-line were arranged so that the speed would be ascertained with a minimum of calculation.

The line and its drum and log-ship are easily made, and

can be attached by clips to the upper rail on the port quarter. In some ships a half-hour and a four-hour sand-glass were carried on the poop, which were used to time the bells and the watches. I made a tiny sand-glass $\frac{1}{8}$ in. high and $\frac{1}{16}$ in. across, which stands in a holder at the side of the log-line reel. The glass was made of two small glass beads, fused together to make a waist.

The Poop Rail.—The hand rail round the poop has twenty-seven two-ball stanchions 2 ft. 6 in. high, painted white. The holes for them may be drilled 1 in. apart in the top rail, but it is advisable to defer putting on this rail until the mizzen rigging has been finished.

INDEX

FIGURE-HEAD OF "CUTTY SARK," 1922.

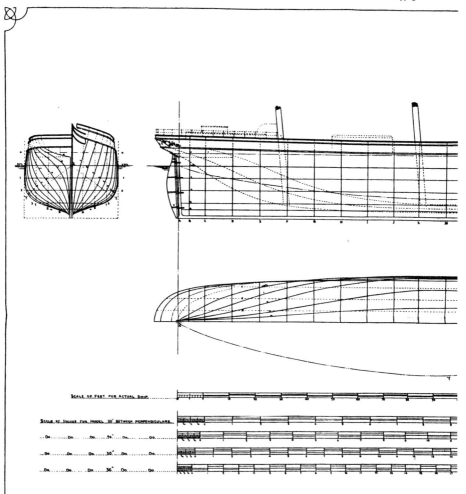

SCALE OF FEET FOR ACTUAL SHIP.

SCALE OF INCHES FOR MODEL 20' BETWEEN PERPENDICULARS.

..Do.......Do.....Do....¼"..Do......Do...

..Do.......Do.....Do....30"..Do......Do...

..Do.......Do.....Do....36"..Do......Do...

LINES FOR MODEL OF CLIPPER SHIP

REGISTERED DIMENSIONS:- LENGTH 212·5 FT., BREADTH 3

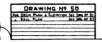

DRAWING Nº 50
FOR DECK PLAN & ELEVATION SEE DRG Nº 51
" SAIL PLAN   SEE DRG Nº 52

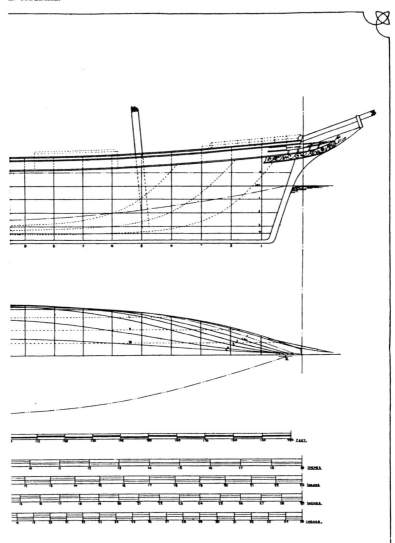

"CUTTY SARK". 921 TONS REGISTER.

FT., REGISTERED DEPTH 21 FT., MOULDED DEPTH 22·5 FT.

HAROLD A UNDERHILL.
GLASGOW.

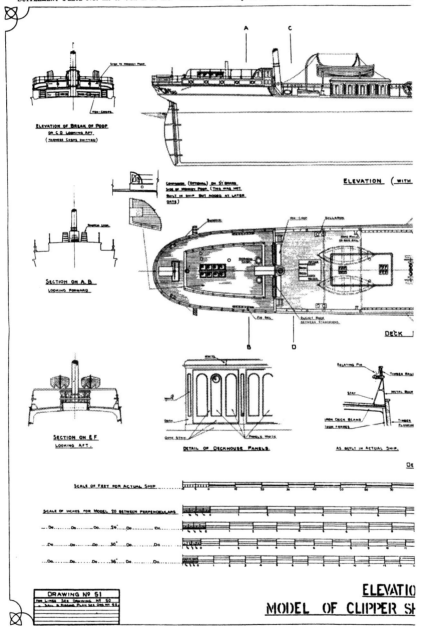

ELEVATION OF BREAK OF POOP
ON C D LOOKING AFT.
(MONKEY COSPS OMITTED)

ELEVATION (WITH

SECTION ON A. B.
LOOKING FORWARD

DECK

SECTION ON E F
LOOKING AFT.

DETAIL OF DECKHOUSE PANELS.

AS BUILT IN ACTUAL SHIP.

SCALE OF FEET FOR ACTUAL SHIP

SCALE OF INCHES FOR MODEL 20 BETWEEN PERPENDICULARS

DRAWING No 51
FOR LINES SEE DRAWING No 50

ELEVATIO
MODEL OF CLIPPER SH

NOTE OF FIREGALE OPEN NO BULKHEAD
BEING FITTED, ENTRANCES TO LOWER FO'CASTLE
BY SMALL HATCH BEHIND LADDER

STARBOARD BULWARKS AND RAILS REMOVED)

PLAN

FOR PLANK BUILT MODEL.

FOR MODEL BUILT FROM SOLID BLOCK.

PLAN SHOWING DECK ARRANGEMENT
WHEN FITTED WITH A DOWN TYPE
WINDLASS. HAWSES BROUGHT THROUGH
DECK.

TAILS OF BULWARK CONSTRUCTION.   NOT TO SCALE.

N & DECK PLAN FOR
IIP "CUTTY SARK". 921 TONS REGISTER.

HAROLD A. UNDERHILL

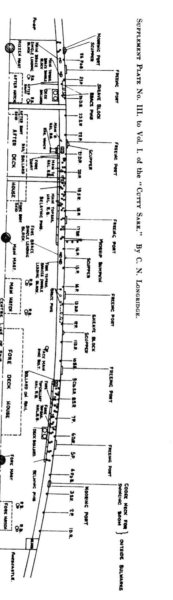

DIAGRAMMATIC LAYOUT OF BULWARKS.

SCALE ⅟₆₀ FULL SIZE

SHROUDS

S	:	MAIN SHROUDS
C	:	CAP BACKSTAY
Tᴍ	:	TOPMAST "
Tᴳ	:	TOPGALLANT "
R	:	ROYAL "
Sᴸ	:	SKYSAIL "

BULWARK STANCHIONS

(NUMBERS REPRESENT STANCHIONS)

D.R.	:	DOUBLE RING
P.	:	PLAIN (i.e. NO RING OR CLEATS)
S.R.	:	SINGLE RING
Cʟ	:	CLEAT
B.	:	BENT.

OTHER ABBREVIATIONS

HAL.	:	HALLIARD
R.B.	:	RING BOLT

NOTE

RING BOLTS FOR TOPSAIL HALLIARDS & RUNNERS ARE IN THE WATERWAYS.

CPSIA information can be obtained at www.ICGtesting.com
Printed in the USA
BVOW011311110512

290002BV00011B/57/P